An Introduction to
Fly Tying

An Introduction to Fly Tying

Pat O'Reilly and Derek Hoskin

Line Illustrations by Keith Linsell

The Crowood Press

First published in 1992 by
The Crowood Press Ltd
Ramsbury, Marlborough
Wiltshire SN8 2HR

British Library Cataloguing in Publication Data

A catalogue record for this book is available from the British Library.

ISBN 1 85223 647 7

I0802130

Edited and designed by
D & N Publishing
DTP & Editorial Services
The Old Surgery
Crowle Road
Lambourn
Berkshire RG16 7NR

Phototypeset by FIDO Imagesetting,
Witney, Oxon

Printed and bound by Times Publishing Group, Singapore

Contents

Acknowledgements   6

Introduction   7

1   Tools and Other Basic Essentials   9

2   Selecting and Storing Materials   15

3   Basic Skills – Tails, Heads and Bodies   24

4   Basic Techniques – Wings and Hackles   39

5   Natural and Artificial Flies   50

6   Shrimps, Nymphs and Pupae   59

7   Wet Flies   71

8   Dry Flies   84

9   Lures   96

    Glossary   105

    Useful Addresses   108

    Further Reading   109

    Index   110

Acknowledgements

There cannot ever have been a fishing book – especially on the subject of fly tying – in which the authors could claim all the ideas as their own. This book is no exception. Over the years we have picked up hints and tips from numerous fly fishers on lake and river bank. To that generous band of colleagues – too many names even to remember, yet too much kindness ever to forget – we are greatly indebted.

We are particularly grateful to the many fly fishers and fly tyers – the beginners and the more advanced – who have joined us on our courses at the West Wales School of Flyfishing, or who supported our charity fund-raising events at various game fairs. We have learned something from each of them. Some have set us thinking with their questions; others have provided answers to problems which have long taxed us. It is this interchange of ideas which makes game angling, and fly tying in particular, such a rewarding pursuit. So, to you all, a heartfelt 'thank you'.

Introduction

Artificial flies are among the cheapest items in the tackle shop, so why do the majority of serious fly fishers spend hour after hour making their own dry flies, wet flies, nymphs and lures? Good question! Could it be that they tie better flies than those available from the local tackle shop? Or do they get some special pleasure from tying their own flies? The answer, in most cases, is both – and you can too with a minimum of tools and materials, as we explain in Chapter 1.

So what are the advantages of tying your own flies? We can think of several. For a start there are far too many disappointments with shop-bought flies. Either the tying falls apart during casting or, even more frustrating, the hook snaps or straightens out under the pressure of a good fish. Yet quality materials

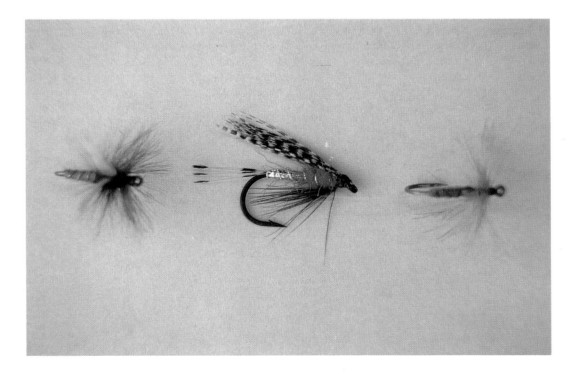

Famous forever: Greenwell's Glory, Peter Ross and Kite's Imperial.

and hooks are quite affordable and readily available if you know what to look for. Therefore, in Chapter 2, we explain how to select good-quality raw materials, without which good flies simply cannot be made. Here you will also find ideas for storing your tools and materials so they do not deteriorate and are readily accessible when needed.

How would you like to be able to design and build your own fly rod? Or set up a small engineering workshop in a spare bedroom to turn out reels exactly as you think they should be made? And what chance is there of doing either? Not a lot! But, once you have mastered the basic skills and techniques of fly tying as covered in Chapters 3 and 4, you can go on to experiment with new materials and patterns and produce flies which no other angler has tried before.

Very few tackle shops hold a comprehensive range of patterns and sizes; yet at times the fish can be very choosy, and you may need just the right pattern to tempt them. We do not pretend that this happens every time you go fishing, of course, but we do know that on average over a season we get far better results by 'matching the hatch' – using close imitations of whatever the trout are feeding on. In Chapter 5 we have included our own views on the important points to consider when designing imitative patterns, and suggestions as to why some lures are much more effective than others. We hope they will help you in your experimenting. Remember, every once in a while a fly tyer hits upon a real winner – a Greenwell's Glory, a Peter Ross or a Kite's Imperial, for example – and their names go down in the annals of angling history, with their patterns copied the world over by grateful fly tyers. We include some ideas worth further experiment, and hope they will set you thinking of others.

Finally – and for many fly tyers that is what the hobby is all about – there is the extra pleasure of deceiving a fish using a fly you have tied yourself. Chapters 6 to 9 will guide you through the tying of a range of nymphs, wet flies, dry flies and lures with useful hints and tips highlighted. Some of these should speed up or simplify the tying process, while others are designed to improve quality or durability.

1 *Tools and Other Basic Essentials*

Fly tying requires few tools, and as they are not expensive it is worth buying the best. Looked after properly, quality tools will last you a lifetime. Not only that, you will find

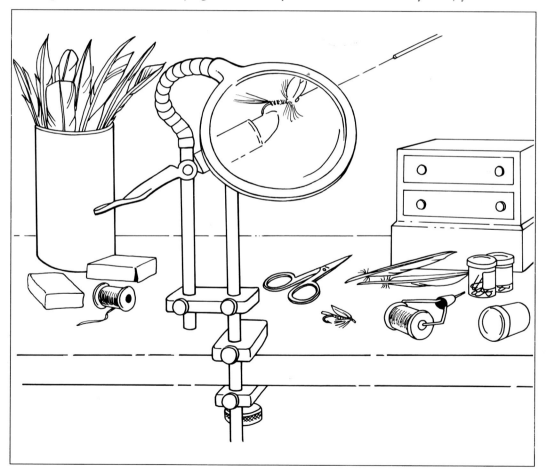

Fig 1 A magnifier fitted on to the vice makes tying tiny dry flies much easier.

With careful planning, a corner of the lounge can become an efficient work area for fly tying.

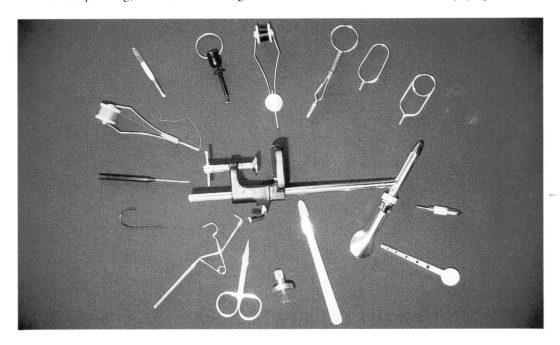

Fly tying tools.

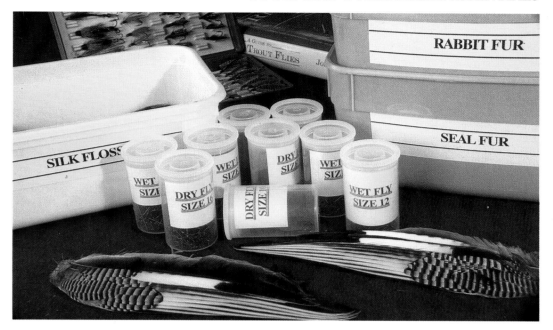

The fly tyer's constant problem: efficient storage. Whether you use ice-cream cartons or a purpose-built storage chest, clear labelling is the key to success.

handling hooks and tying materials so much easier when using first class tools, and this will help you become a skilful fly tyer more quickly. The same applies to materials, and with these you can make a good start with just a small range, gradually adding a few more exotic materials when you come across a bargain.

We do have to admit right away, however, that if you do not think from the outset about organizing your tying facility, even the modest starter kit we recommend in this book can easily become an unmanageable mess. Of course, not everyone has the temperament to set up and operate an elaborate storage system where there is a special place for everything; but, without some sort of organization, tools soon get lost and materials become tangled or spoilt.

Therefore, we recommend a simple approach based on the minimum of tools and materials, a compact yet well-illuminated work area, and storage arrangements which adequately protect both your tools and your tying materials.

THE WORK AREA

To work efficiently you must be reasonably comfortable. Ideally, you should be able to leave a job and return to it later without worrying about what has happened to it while you were away. But how many fly tyers live in such an ideal world? In many homes space is at a premium, and you are probably lucky if you have a fly-tying corner, let alone a room for this purpose. However, even if you do

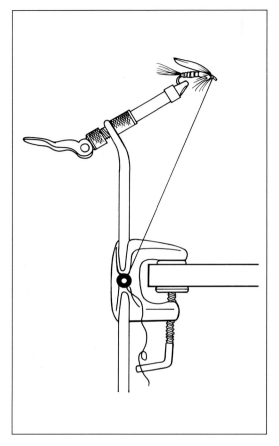

Fig 2   A rubber grommet is fitted on some vices to hold the thread securely. This leaves both hands free for preparing materials.

just have a corner of the lounge or dining room there is a lot you can do to make it an effective facility.

The Fly-Tying Bench

Apart from being at a comfortable height for working, the most important requirement of a tying bench is that it should be sturdy – a bench or table that wobbles about is useless

for the delicate task of tying flies. A simple table or desk 26–28in tall will be fine. On the surface we always place a large sheet of pale card which can be replaced at little cost when it gets soiled or damaged. Not only does this protect the bench top but it also provides an ideal background against which to view your work.

As for seating, a variable-height office chair of the swivel type is ideal, especially if the back rest can also be adjusted. We like the type without arms, but this is largely a matter of personal preference.

Lighting and Magnification

A well-lit work area is absolutely essential. You will probably need a lamp on which you can adjust the direction of the beam. Fluorescent lighting is not advisable, especially if you live in an area where the mains supply is prone to irregular fluctuations; an ordinary filament lamp will flicker less and reduce the strain on your eyes. A 60-watt angled lamp secured to one end of the bench is an ideal arrangement.

For very fine work, such as fitting wings on tiny dry flies, many people find additional magnification a great help. When buying a magnifier, either buy a vice at the same time or take your vice to the shop and try the magnifier on it. Make sure that it fits well and can be adjusted to give the clearance you will need when tying flies.

CHOOSING YOUR FLY-TYING TOOLS

Fly tying is a well-developed art, and tool design has evolved to the point where price is a reasonably good guide to quality: you only get what you pay for. There is some virtue in checking price competitiveness, of course, but if your local tackle dealer is a fly tyer there are obvious benefits in buying locally where you can get on-the-spot advice from an expert.

The Tying Vice

A good fly-tying vice is an investment. The vice must hold the hook really securely whilst you are tying: any vice which allows the hook to slip about is virtually useless. If you are working to a tight budget, put most of your money into a first-class vice and you will not regret it. Of the many designs on the market the most popular, and we think the best, is the lever-operated type. The height can be adjusted, the fly can be set to any angle you want, and the hardened steel jaws can be made to grip firmly hooks of varying sizes from the tiniest of trout hooks to quite substantial salmon 'irons'.

If you are right-handed, fix the vice to your bench just to the left of where you will sit, and set the jaws to face towards your right. Initially, adjust the height so that the hook is about 6in from the surface of the desk. If you find this is too close to your face then lower the vice a little (or raise the height of your seat if it is adjustable).

A useful attachment on some tying vices is a rubber grommet. You can use this to secure the tying thread if for any reason you have to cease work part of the way through tying a fly. If your vice does not have a grommet you can make one with two rubber tap washers screwed to the edge of your bench alongside the vice.

Another handy gadget which can be fitted on most vices is a spring for holding materials which have been secured to the hook and which will be used later in the tying sequence. For example, certain types of nymphs are tied with feather fibres wound over a body of fine wire. The feather can be held out of the way by means of the spring attachment while you are building up the wire underbody.

Scissors

Good scissors are essential. For cutting wire and tinsel you will need a strong pair of clippers or straight scissors, and for trimming fine fur or hackles, a smaller pair kept really sharp will make life a lot easier. Some fly tyers prefer curved scissors for fine trimming work; others insist that straight scissors are better. We prefer a pair of each; but, whatever you choose make sure they are razor sharp.

Bobbin Holder

Bobbin holders carry a small spool of tying thread which you can draw off as you need it. Although not essential they are a real boon to people who send spools of thread rolling and unravelling across the floor frequently! If you choose not to use a bobbin holder, then the rubber grommet referred to above becomes invaluable.

Hackle Pliers

These are made of spring steel and are used for gripping hackle feathers when winding them on to a hook, for example, to represent the legs of an insect. Pliers with serrated jaws are fine for handling larger hackles (as long as they are well made so that the jaws actually meet!) Rubber tubing slipped over the jaws will ensure that even quite fine hackles can be held firmly without risk of them being cut by the metal jaws.

Another style of hackle pliers derives from the miniature circuit-test probes used in the electronics industry. These plastic-bodied pliers are held shut by a small compression spring. They work very well on both large and small hackles.

Dubbing Needle

This is something you can make quite easily. Drill a small hole in a broken-off toothbrush handle or similar length of plastic. Next, mix a little epoxy resin using the eyed end of a darning needle, and finally push this adhesive-coated end of the needle into the hole in the plastic handle. Once the epoxy resin has set, use this tool for pricking out fibres of fur from the bodies of flies and nymphs to represent their legs.

The dubbing needle can also be used for applying tiny drops of varnish to the heads of finished flies, and for clearing the varnish from the eye of the hook if you have been over liberal with the head varnish.

Craft-Knife or Scalpel

A small craft-knife or a surgical scalpel with spare blades is useful for cutting thin plastic sheet or polythene to shape. You can also use this tool for cutting off the tying thread once a fly has been completed. You simply hold the thread tight and touch it with the scalpel where it emerges from the head of the fly; the thread will part cleanly while the hackles, which are not under tension, simply move back out of the way. When not in use, a flattened piece of plastic pipe can be fitted over the blade as a protective scabbard.

A very sharp penknife is almost as good and does have the advantage that the blade can be folded away safely when not in use.

Whip Finish Tool

The whip finish is a neat and secure way of completing the head of a fly, and there is a tool available to help with this task. In our experience it takes no longer to learn to tie the whip finish by hand than to learn to handle this tool effectively. However, some people find it difficult to master the manual technique, and for them this tool is invaluable.

In Chapter 3 we show you how to make the whip finish both with and without a whip-finish tool.

STORAGE AND CARE OF YOUR TOOLS

As long as cutting blades and vice jaws are properly protected, fly-tying tools need only be kept away from the damp and they will last indefinitely. Any small, strong box will do as a tool store, but if you do travel around the country frequently in order to fish in different venues, you may want to take your tools and a few basic materials with you so that you can tie up flies which will suit local conditions. Whether you decide on a plastic ice-cream carton or a polished mahogany chest, your tools can be held securely in place if you line the box with plastic foam and then cut out cavities to suit each tool. (You can use your scalpel for this job!)

The only regular maintenance necessary is the sharpening of scissor blades, which can be done quite easily on a fine-grade oil stone. If you prefer to use a very sharp penknife rather than a scalpel then a small oil stone kept in your fly-tying kit will allow you to keep the blade really sharp. Scalpel blades are relatively inexpensive so you will find it is hardly worth the effort involved in trying to re-sharpen them.

2 Selecting and Storing Materials

With the exception of hooks, the materials needed for most fly patterns cost very little. For example, enough good quality silk and feathers to tie 1,000 Black Gnat dry flies will cost you less than the price of thirty shop-bought flies. But the problem remains: how do you tell good quality from bad? The answer lies both in the raw materials and in the tying.

Once people know you tie your own flies, you may be inundated with gifts of feathers, furs, silks and hooks from well-wishers, which it is difficult to refuse. Old furs are often quite all right, but usually by the time you have discarded the rusty hooks and moth-eaten feathers there is not a lot left – materials, particularly those of natural rather than man-made origin, degenerate with age.

Furs and feathers, the basic ingredients of traditional flies.

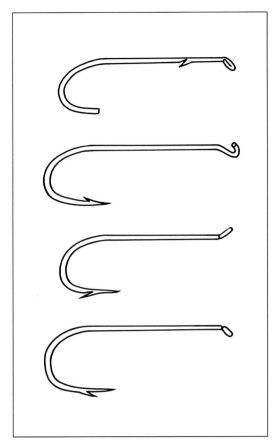

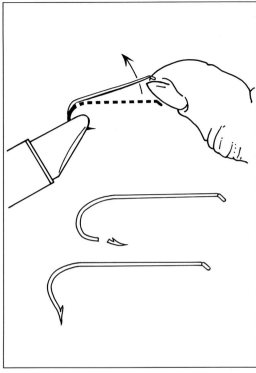

Fig 4   Test each hook – to destruction if necessary – before a trout does.

Fig 3   Manufacturing defects: few suppliers inspect each individual hook.

Birds and furry mammals that meet untimely ends in road accidents are always welcomed, of course, by those fly tyers willing and able to deal with the business of skinning and curing. In the Further Reading chapter at the back of this book you will find details of books on collecting and curing your own fly-tying materials.

Hooks and materials really must be of a good quality to start with, and they need careful handling and storage if they are to

remain in good condition until you get round to using them.

SELECTING AND TESTING HOOKS

Hook making seems to be in an in-between state – not quite a science, but too repetitive to be classed as art. One thing is for sure: there is a lot which can go wrong between wire and finished hook. Since reliability is as important as design, we have no hesitation in recommending that you buy hooks of the very best quality. That means, at the present time, that you have to pay a little extra for the

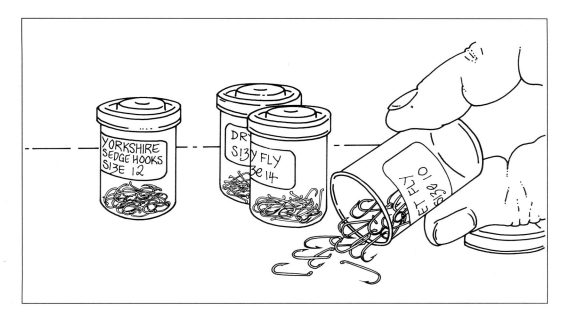

Fig 5　35mm film canisters make ideal hook stores.

care, meticulous attention to detail, and thoroughness of inspection necessary to produce the best.

Some very strange things can and do go wrong in the manufacturing process, resulting in hooks varying from poor quality to those which are totally unusable. Some faults can be spotted at once. Avoid hooks with the following common defects:

1.　Point blunt or bent over, preventing good penetration.
2.　Eye not properly closed, so the leader can slip through the gap and become detached.
3.　Barb cut so deep that the point could easily be snapped off under pressure from a fish.
4.　Barb angling steeply away from point, thus resisting penetration.
5.　Barb cut on the outside of the bend instead of the inside.

You will note that many of the common faults are associated with the barb. We have seen very few faulty barbless hooks – just one more reason for fishing with these hooks.

It is impossible to tell just by looking at a hook whether the steel is too brittle or too soft and, despite manufacturers testing samples from each batch, the occasional mistake can slip through. It may not happen often, but it is best to be on the safe side: test each hook before you tie a fly on it.

To test a hook insert it into the tying vice and tighten the jaws securely. With your thumb-nail, pull upwards on the eye of the hook and then let it slip back. The hook should sound with a bright metallic 'ping', the note depending upon the size of the hook. If the hook is faulty it will do one of two things: either it will break off at the barb, signifying that the steel has not been tempered sufficiently, or the gape will widen

A range of threads and tinsels. Note the use of Blu-tack to secure loose ends.

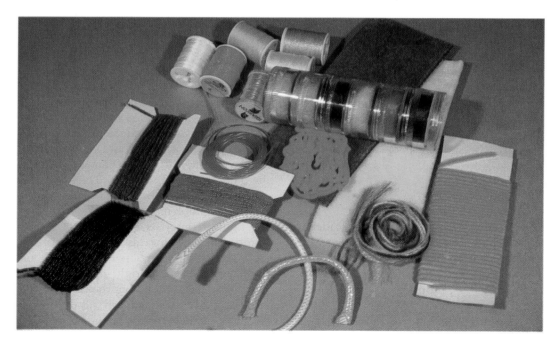

The range of colours available in synthetic materials has led to a new era in fly-tying innovation.

Varnishes, pens and paints are all used in the finishing of certain fly patterns.

permanently, which means that the steel is far too soft. Hook testing is time well spent, as either of these occurrences could have cost you a good fish!

Throughout this book we refer to specific styles of hooks. We have chosen to refer to the Partridge range because we find them to be of consistently high quality and available in an extensive range of styles, sizes and weights. Other manufacturers' nearest equivalents can, of course, be used, but bitter experience has taught us not to take chances with this most crucial item of the fly fisher's tackle.

Save your 35mm film canisters – the see-through ones are especially good – since with suitable stick-on labels they make excellent damp-proof hook storage containers. They are particularly good for double and treble hooks which tend to burst their paper packets.

STORING AND TAKING CARE OF MATERIALS

While synthetic materials such as tying threads and silks need only be protected from the damaging rays of direct sunlight, furs and feathers are prone to vermin and decay if they are not properly treated. Many of these materials also contain natural oils which gradually evaporate, leaving the materials dry and brittle and more difficult to handle; this process is accelerated if they are stored in a very warm room. Keep natural materials away from damp. To help preserve them and to

L3B–Captain Hamilton Dry Fly Hooks (Up Eye)
Identical with L3A but an up eye.

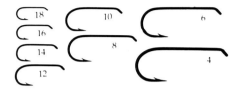

H1A–Captain Hamilton Nymph Hooks
For longer nymphs, lightweight lures and streamer flies. Captain Hamilton wide gape and about 2½x long on middleweight wire.

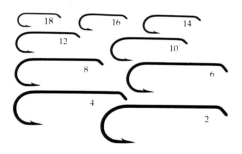

L2A–Captain Hamilton Wet Fly Hooks
For lighter wet flies and nymphs, and strong dry flies with down eye.

R1A–Double Limerick Hooks
Identical with J1A but a double version and therefore slightly shorter in body length. For traditional wet flies and point flies. A really strong hook.

CS20–Mike Weaver Arrowpoint (Barbless) Dry Fly Hooks
For all types of dry flies and floating nymphs. Unique barbless arrowpoint hooks which hold just as well as barbed hooks. Otherwise modelled on E6A design.

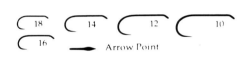

K2B–Yorkshire Sedge Hooks
For sedge pupa and larva, shrimp and grub patterns, and 'upside down' flies. Slight up eye aids hooking and fine curved shank.

Fig 6   Partridge hook profiles.

ward off attack by mites and moths, crumble a few flakes of naphthalene (moth-balls) into each container.

One litre (and larger) ice-cream containers are ideal for storing furs. Some of these containers are translucent, however, and should not be left for long periods in direct sunlight. Small feathers are best kept flat in grip-seal polythene bags. You could then keep all your cock hackles, for example, bagged separately but stored together in the same ice-cream container. Peacock tails, ostrich plumes and other long feathers are best stored in tall jars or laid flat between stiff cardboard in drawers so they do not get damaged.

Tying Tip

The slots in spools soon wear and no longer hold the material securely; a small piece of Blu-Tack solves this problem.

Spools of silk, fine wire and tinsel can soon become a complete mess if left to roll about in the bottom of your tool box. They are best packed in a container with a tight fitting lid. Add a piece of foam plastic to make a snug fit – you can always reduce the size of the foam as you add to your collection of spools.

A BEGINNER'S BASIC MATERIALS LIST

All of the flies mentioned in this book can be tied with the economy list of materials given below. Sometimes we have altered the tying recipe from that given by the inventor of the fly, but we have found that our attempts at standardizing on a restricted list of materials have in no way diminished the fish-catching properties of these flies.

In the list we have included brand names which we recommend; this is not to imply any criticism of brands which we have not mentioned and which may well be equally suitable.

Hooks

1. Fine wire up-eye dry fly hooks in sizes 10, 12, 14 and 16 (for example, Partridge type L3B).
2. Standard shank wet fly forged down-eye in sizes 8, 10, 12 and 14 (for example, Partridge type L2A).
3. Long shank down-eyed nymph hooks in sizes 8, 10 and 12 (for example, Partridge type H1A).
4. Yorkshire Sedge grub hooks in sizes 12 and 14 (for example Partridge type K2B).
5. Mike Weaver arrowpoint (barbless) hooks in sizes 10 to 16 (for example, Partridge type CS20).
6. Double hooks in sizes 10 and 12 (for example, Partridge type R1A).
7. Treble hooks in sizes 10 and 12 (for example, Partridge type 3BL).

Tying Thread

Fine pre-waxed tying thread in black, white, brown, red, yellow and olive.

Ribbing Materials

1. Flat silver tinsel – the heavyweight type is best. Get medium-width tinsel to begin with; you can add other widths to your collection in due course.
2. Medium, oval silver tinsel.
3. Flat gold tinsel.
4. Oval gold tinsel.
5. Fine gold wire.
6. Fine and medium silver Lurex.
7. Fine and medium gold Lurex.

Silk Floss

Skeins of silk floss in black, white, brown, red, orange, yellow and olive.

Wool

1. Nylon baby wool in white, orange, red and green.
2. Lamb's wool (can be collected from barbed-wire fences!)

Chenille

Fine chenille in black, white, yellow, green and orange.

Furs

1. Seal or seal substitute in black, brown, orange and olive.
2. Squirrel in natural grey, black and orange.
3. Rabbit in natural grey.
4. Deer in natural, white and black.

Tying Tip

Complete golden pheasant capes, without tippets or toppings, are inexpensive and provide useful feathers in a wide range of colours.

Feathers

1. Cockerel hackles in black, brown, red, blue and olive. (Gradually build up a range of cock hackles, including badger, coch-y-bonddhu, furnace, ginger, greenwell, grizzle, cree and honey dun.)
2. Hen hackles in black and brown.
3. Partridge, barred teal and guinea-fowl breast feathers.

4. Pairs of wings from blackbird, mallard and coot.
5. Cock and hen pheasant tail feathers.
6. Ostrich fibres in brown and white.
7. Bronze peacock herls.
8. Golden pheasant tippets and toppings.

Plastics and Other Man-Made Materials

1. Heavy-gauge polythene bags or sheet.
2. Fine woven silver mylar tubing.
3. Heavy-pile nylon carpet off-cuts of various colours.
4. Polythene balls.
5. Old nylon stockings.
6. Celire varnish in clear and black.
7. Wax block.

Save any scraps of man-made materials you think might be useful, and add waterproof, quick-drying pens and paints to your collection as the opportunity arises.

EXTENDING YOUR FLY-TYING FACILITY

It won't be long before you want to design patterns of your own, either to imitate a particular insect or to attract fish in unusual circumstances – for example in difficult lighting conditions. To do this you will need to extend your collection of materials. One of the biggest problems you will meet as your collection of fly tying materials grows is how to find what you want.

One way of keeping a growing collection of materials under control is to store on your tying bench only those materials you use frequently – threads, tinsels, furs and commonly-used feathers, for example. Then store everything else in numbered boxes (or better still, in labelled drawers in a cupboard if you have the luxury of plenty of space).

Organization: the key to finding the materials you want. Frequently used materials are ready to hand, while less common ones are filed away in boxes or cupboards.

Organization is the Key

So that you don't end up rummaging through every box when you want to find a particular item, keep a list of the contents of each. Alphabetical lists on index cards may seem rather beaurocratic, but they can save a lot of time in the long run. But remember, whatever the system you eventually decide will suit you best, it will let you down if you don't put things back in the right place as soon as you have finished with them. We know: we've wasted many hours ourselves hunting for a particular type of feather or colour of silk which wasn't there when it should have been!

3 Basic Skills – Tails, Heads and Bodies

This chapter will help you develop the essential skills of fly tying. Follow the illustrated examples and you will learn to use your tools to tie a range of commonly used materials.

ANATOMY OF AN ARTIFICIAL FLY

It is unrealistic to talk about the 'correct' dimensions and proportions for wet flies, dry flies and nymphs. For one thing, natural insects vary from one specimen to another, and there are occasions when exaggerating some aspect of a fly – making it longer, fatter, shorter or slimmer – can trigger a trout into selecting it in preference to the competing naturals on or in the water.

In this book we show the proportions which are generally about right for most purposes, however, if you look carefully at flies tied by the experts, you will see how they vary these proportions occasionally to obtain particular effects. For example, the length of the body of a salmon fly can be altered for fishing in high-, medium- or low-water conditions. Lures can be almost any shape. Fortunately the basic tying methods are much the same regardless of actual pattern, although the nature of each particular material limits what you can do with it.

We recommend that you tackle each new technique on a size 10 hook, but once you have mastered a technique you should try varying the amounts of materials to suit larger and smaller hooks. If you are interested in competitive fly fishing you will have to tie flies which comply with the maximum dimensions permitted in international competitions.

GETTING STARTED

Make a start by fixing a size 10 forged (wet fly) hook into your vice. When using barbed or plain barbless hooks, the point can be concealed within the jaws of the vice, thus avoiding the risk of catching your tying thread on the point of the hook. With certain styles of hooks – for example, the Mike Weaver arrowpoint types which are flattened in the horizontal plane – you will have to secure the hook at the bend. Double and treble hooks can only be secured by one of their points, so you will have to learn to handle exposed points on occasion.

The next step is to thread your bobbin holder and apply wax to your tying thread. (Even ready-waxed thread seems to benefit from an extra coat of wax immediately before use.) Place the thread over a block of wax and hold it in place with a thumb. Now pull down so that the thread slides smoothly over the wax. Friction will melt the wax. Repeat two more times to ensure that the thread is well covered. You are now ready for business.

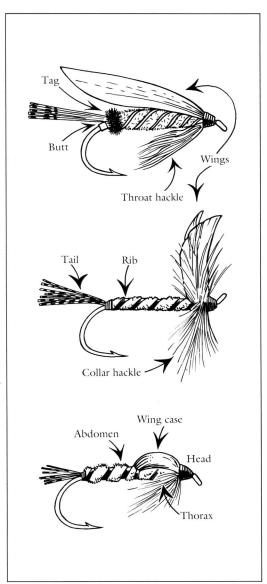

Fig 7   Typical proportions for wet fly, dry fly and nymph.

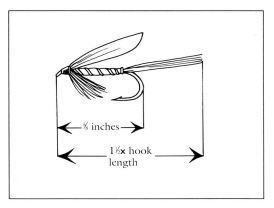

Fig 8   Maximum hook and fly dimensions for international competitions.

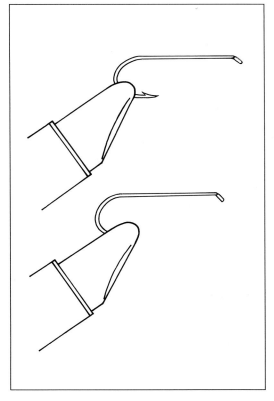

Fig 9   Alternative methods of mounting for conventional barbed hooks.

The Foundation Layer

The first stage when making any fly is to wrap turns of waxed thread tightly around the hook shank. In theory these turns need not be tightly spaced unless you are going to cover them with a tinsel body material. In practice we recommend closely wound turns always for improved durability: your fly body will not rotate about the hook shank if it is built upon a firm foundation.

The foundation layer should run from just behind the eye to where the hook bend starts. To start the foundation, hold the thread vertically against the near side of the hook shank, with the free end below and the bobbin holder above. Take the bobbin holder behind and under the hook shank to complete one turn. As you complete the turn,

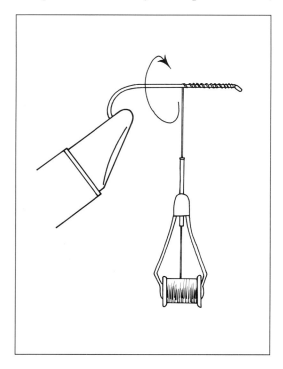

Fig 10 Winding on the foundation layer.

bring the thread backwards slightly to trap the free end of the thread.

When you reach a position directly above the hook point, cut off the free end of the thread close to the hook shank. Add two or three more turns and leave the bobbin holder hanging; its weight will hold everything securely in place.

Tying Tip

Hold the free end of the thread out at an angle of about 45 degrees to the hook shank, and continue winding turns of thread back towards the bend. Each turn will slip down the sloping thread to nestle up tightly against the preceding one. In this way you can wind turns very quickly indeed and still get a really neat foundation layer.

TAILS

Any trailing appendage at the rear of an artificial fly is called a tail. Some do indeed represent the tails of small fish or tadpoles, or the setae of insects. With lure patterns, tails are often added to provide a pulsating action suggesting life. Fortunately, the method of attaching tails varies little with the type of material used, and the examples below should provide the experience you need to handle other materials.

Feather Fibre and Feather Slip Tails

Let us start with a tail made from feather fibres. Take a cock hackle and pull off the soft downy 'flue' from the base. Now draw down the fibres so they stick out at right angles. Grip four or five long fibres between your thumb and forefinger and pull them away from the stalk. Transfer the fibres to your left

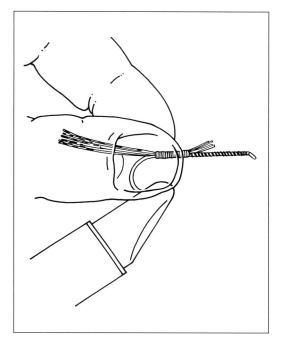

Fig 11 Always ensure the tail material is mounted directly above the hook shank.

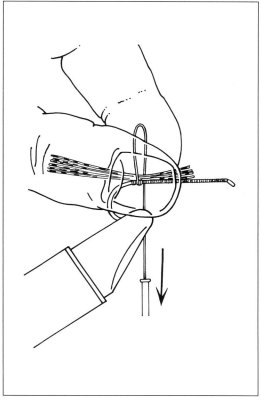

Fig 12 The 'pinch-and-loop' technique.

hand and hold them along the top of the hook shank, gripping both the fibres and the hook shank.

The next step is to secure the tail using the pinch-and-loop technique. Raise the bobbin holder so that the thread is drawn upwards on the near side of the hook, pulling firmly so that the thread can be trapped between your left thumb and the hook shank. Now make a loop with the thread above the tail and bring it down on the far side of the hook shank, again trapping it against the shank with your left forefinger. Pull down on the thread so that the loop is drawn down tight on top of the tail. Do not release the grip with your left hand. Repeat this process making two more loops above the tail, so that it is secured with three neatly butting turns. Now you can let go! Trim off the spare tail material.

Feather slip tails are tied in exactly the same way, but the individual feather fibres should remain married together. Indeed, you can even marry different coloured slips together. Red and white goose wing feathers are used in the Parmachene Belle, for example.

Take a pair of similar sized red and white wing feathers, both taken either from the left or from the right wings. (Do not use feathers from opposite wings.) From the white feather use your dubbing needle to select a slip of three or four fibres, and using your scissors cut them free from the stalk. Now take a slip from the corresponding position on the red feather. Place the base of the white slip, with the dull side towards you, between your left thumb and forefinger. Position the red slip immediately above it, again with the dull side towards you. With your right hand, stroke the slips away from the base and the little Velcro-like hooks will intermesh and marry together. Finally, place the composite slip on top of the hook shank and secure with three pinch-and-loop turns.

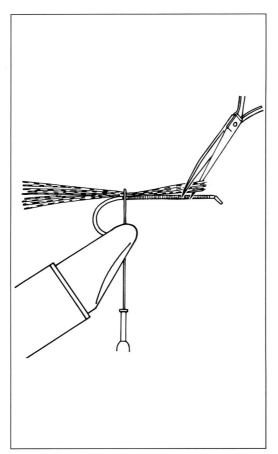

Fig 13 Trimming off the surplus tail material.

Hair Tails

Some large dry flies and many lures make use of hair tails. Deer hair is particularly popular because it has hollow fibres which aid buoyancy. Trim a pinch of fibres from a cured skin, and tease out the soft base hairs. Align the ends of the fibres before holding them in position above the foundation layer. Make four full turns of thread to secure the tail in position. Wind the thread three-quarters of the way along the hook shank and lock with three more tight turns. Trim off the excess tail material.

Marabou Tails

Originally taken from the marabou stork, the feather we call marabou now comes from the legs of a turkey. Dyed in many hues, it wafts through the water in a most tantalizing manner when you apply a jerky retrieve to your fly line. Lures such as nobblers and puppies owe much of their effectiveness to their marabou tails.

To tie a marabou tail, snip off a bunch of fibres and hold them over the prepared hook shank so that the tail is about one and a half times as long as the shank. (Longer tails get more attention, but can result in 'short takes' as the trout seize the tail without engulfing the hook.) Use two pinch-and-loop turns to secure the tail before running the thread up the shank to lock down the marabou butts, trimming off the excess well before the head position.

Other Tail Materials

Wool, polyester, floss silk and many other man-made materials can be used as tails. The basic pinch-and-loop tying-in method will ensure that the tail does not rotate to reduce the effective gape of the hook.

1 Take the bobbin holder in the right hand, and use the first and second fingers of your left hand to form a figure 4 with the thread.

2 Push the first finger over and round the hook shank five times, trapping the free end of the thread each time.

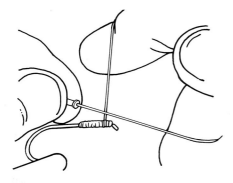

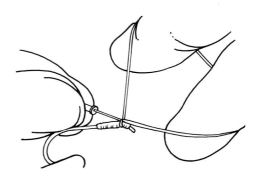

3 Pull the loop as small as you can, then...

4 Slip your bobbin into the loop in place of your fingers; pull down, remove the needle...tighten fully...finished.

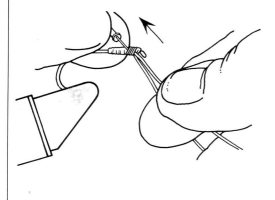

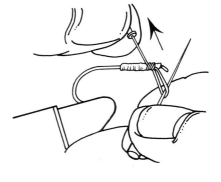

Fig 14 Making a whip finish.

A marabou tail provides the centre of attraction in this nobbler lure.

HEADS

The head of the fly is where we finish off the tying. Heads should be small, neat and securely finished. Body, hackle and wing materials are all tied in at the head, and we need to do this without building up too much bulk. If the head is bulky not only will the fly look ugly, but the setting of the hook could be impeded.

To build up a head, wind on neat turns of tying thread into a nice, rounded shape. Some fly tyers use half-hitch knots to secure the end of the thread, but this never leaves a really neat finish. Instead, use the whip finish, which can be done by hand or with a simple whip-finish tool.

Making the Whip Finish

Form a triangle with the tying thread, twisting your hand round so the thread lies along the top of the hook shank. Wind four full turns, trapping the free end of the thread each time. Pull back on the bobbin holder to reduce the loop around your fingers, and carefully slip your dubbing needle into the loop before withdrawing your fingers. Be sure

to keep tension on the loop at all times. Finally, pull all the spare thread from the loop and withdraw the dubbing needle, giving it a final tighten and snipping off the spare thread.

A whip-finishing tool can be used in place of your fingers. The process is as described above, except that you do not need to swap your fingers for the dubbing needle as the whip-finish tool does the whole job.

Practice whip finishing on a bare hook shank until you are really skilled at it; the whip finish is such a useful technique, both in fly dressing and in the repair of many items of fishing tackle.

BODIES

The body of a natural insect is the part from which the trout obtains sustenance. Other parts may be important in attracting attention, but once the trout approaches its prey, its interest is likely to be in the meal rather than the packaging. For this reason, we think it is worth learning to tie credible representations of insect bodies. There is a wide variety to choose from – some bodies are furry, some are shiny and many are divided into segments. We can copy the size, form and texture of real insects using a range of materials and tying methods.

Tying Thread Bodies

Having wound on the foundation layer (do not bother with a tail while you are practising), simply return towards the eye of the hook, adding closely butting turns. For a slim body, two layers will be enough; meatier creatures can be copied by building up three or more layers, stopping each layer short of the previous one to obtain a neatly tapering body.

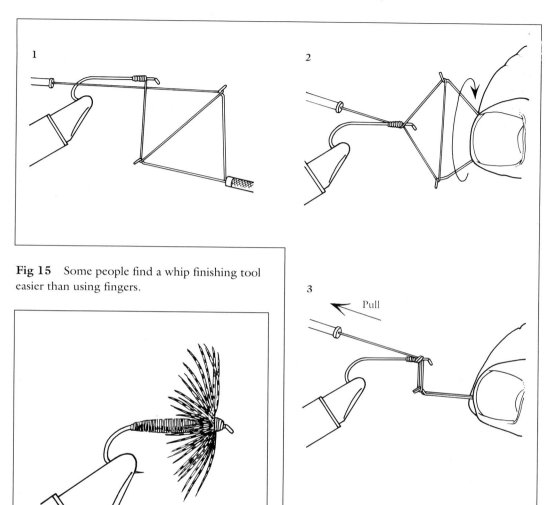

1

2

3

Pull

Fig 15 Some people find a whip finishing tool easier than using fingers.

Fig 16 A tying thread body is used in the simple, but very effective, Partridge and Orange.

Silk Bodies

Silk floss is good if you need to build up a thick body. Pinch and loop a 6in length at the tail position. Now run the tying thread back to the head before winding a body with the silk floss. Cream silk floss is ideal for tying the bodies of Mayflies.

Tying Tip

Whenever you add in a new material, tie it on top of the hook shank; otherwise the extra bulk at the point of tying will reduce the effective gape of the hook and so reduce hooking capability.

Ribbing

Having prepared your hook, tie in a length of gold wire and then a length of olive silk floss at the tail position. Wind the tying thread forward to the head position. Now build up a floss body, locking off the silk at the head position. You are now ready to add the ribbing which will represent the segments of the fly body. Wind the ribbing in six or eight equally spaced turns along the body. Lock the gold wire with two pinch-and-loop turns, trim off the excess material and admire your handiwork. Did you wind your ribbing in the same direction as the silk floss? If so, the wire will have bedded down deeply, making a body with very distinctive segments. Winding the ribbing in the opposite direction to the floss gives a more visible rib and less distinct segments. Which method is best? Look closely at the insect you are copying and choose whichever method gives greatest realism.

Feather Fibre Bodies

Some feathers have large fibres that can be used singly or in small bunches to build up fly bodies. The Pheasant Tail Nymph – probably the most popular imitation of upwinged nymphs – uses fibres from the centre tail feathers of the brown cock pheasant.

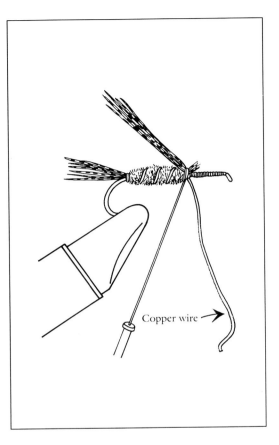

Copper wire →

Fig 17   Tying in the wing case of a Pheasant Tail nymph.

Tying Tip

As with floss bodies, when ribbing feather fibre bodies winding the ribbing in the opposite direction to the fibre will make the body more durable and the ribbing stand out more clearly.

If, however, you want to produce a strongly segmented body, wind the ribbing in the same direction as the body material, so that it can sink down between the body fibres.

Pull away six fibres from the feather stalk, align the tips and trim away the base stalk. Lock the fibres on to the foundation layer at the tail position, leaving a tail of half the shank length. Also lock in a length of fine copper wire which will add weight to the nymph as well as serving as ribbing.

Run the tying thread back to the thorax position before winding the fibre body up to the same point. Wind on the body ribbing. If you have chosen very long fibres and a small hook size, you may be able to continue with the same fibres for the thorax; otherwise tie in a new set of fibres at this point. Take the tying thread forward to the head position. Next build up a humped thorax with the copper wire, tying the wire off at the beginning of the thorax. Pull the wing-case fibres forward over the thorax, and secure at the head position with the tying thread.

Tying Tip

Most nymphs have shiny or translucent wing cases, so tie the wing-case material so that when you fold it forward the shiny side will be outwards.

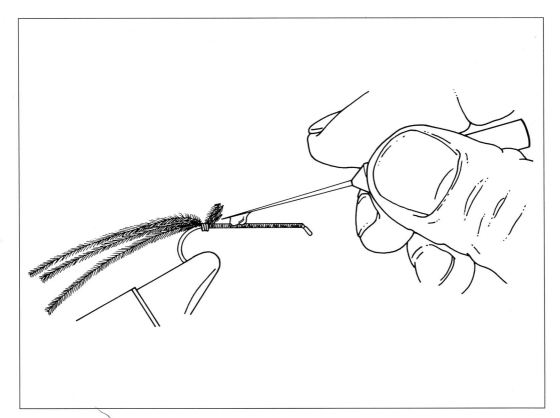

Fig 18   A smear of varnish along the foundation layer will add strength to bodies tied with a fragile peacock herl.

Ribbing a dry fly. The body segments are more pronounced if the ribbing is wound in the same direction as the body material.

Variations on a theme: four patterns of Pheasant Tail nymphs.

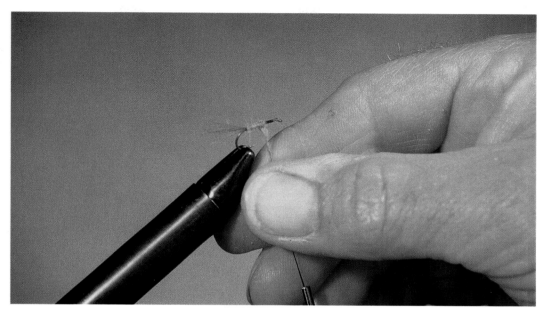

Dubbing a fur body.

Mylar bodies closely resemble the scales on the flanks of small fishes.

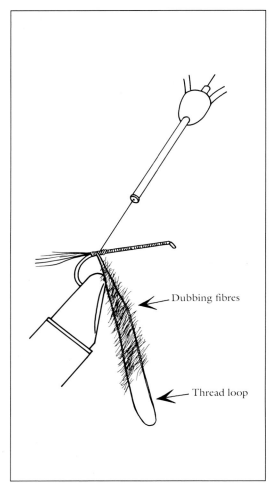

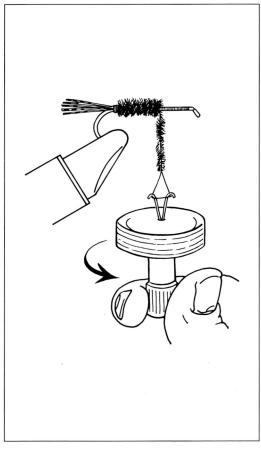

Fig 20   Using the dubbing tool.

Fig 19   Making a dubbing loop.

Trim off the spare materials, add a neat head and your nymph is ready for action.

Peacock Herl and Chenille Bodies

Peacock herl can also be used as a body material; it is the basis of the Coch-y-Bonddhu, the Black and Peacock Spider and many other traditional patterns.

Tying Tip
To reduce unwanted bulk at the point of tying in, pull off the chenille fibres from the last ⅛ in of their centre core and tie down just the core itself.

Having run a foundation layer from eye to hook bend, take half a dozen peacock tail fibres, align them and trim them to equal length. Pinch and loop the points in at the hook bend. Now give the foundation layer a coat of varnish using your dubbing needle. Twist the herls together with the tying thread to form a 'rope', and wind a body from bend to head. Lock in the peacock herl rope at the head position, trim off the excess and leave until the varnish has dried. Despite using fragile peacock herls, you have been able to tie a very durable body which sparkles as light reflects from its multi-coloured fibres.

Chenille, an artificial material very similar to peacock herl rope, can be secured in just the same way to produce an extremely durable body.

Dubbed Bodies

A dubbed body is made by using the tying thread to trap individual fibres of material against the prepared hook shank. These fibres then stick out at all angles and, with a dry fly, create many tiny depressions in the surface. Fished beneath the surface, a dubbed body will trap tiny air bubbles giving the fly body a translucent appearance not unlike some hatching nymphs.

> **Tying Tip**
>
> If you have difficulty with dubbing, get one of the simple dubbing tools now available. Having made a dubbing loop, attach the tool and spin it like a top. Now wind on the dubbing as given in the instructions.

Begin as usual with a foundation layer of waxed thread. Start with a few pinches of rabbit fur and rub it with a finger in a circular motion in the palm of your hand – this is to mix the fibres thoroughly. Now take a small pinch of fur and twist it on to the waxed thread. Roll it in one direction only, sliding it up towards the hook shank. Add more dubbing material to create a furry rope. Next, wind the rope on to the hook in neat turns to build up whatever body shape you need. Once you have finished making the body, secure the tying and prick out a few of the long 'guard hairs' to represent the legs of your fly.

Mylar Tubing Bodies

Woven mylar tubing makes superb fry imitations: the weave reflects light like the scales on the flanks of a fish.

Cut to length, and with the inner cotton core removed, the mylar tubing can be threaded on to the hook shank, tied down and varnished at each end for added security.

Deer Hair Bodies

Hollow deer hair fibres float very well even in turbulent water and are the basis of many 'spun' fly bodies.

> **Tying Tip**
>
> Add a touch of varnish to the mylar tube at intervals equal to the required body length. Once the varnish is dry you can cut the tube to length without the risk of the ends fraying.

Prepare the hook as usual before cutting a pinch of deer fibres and pulling out the soft under-fur. (Do not discard the under-fur: it makes useful dubbing material for nymph bodies.)

Trim off the tips so that you have a bunch of fibres about 1in long. Place the fibres along the hook shank at the tail position. Make two pinch-and-loop turns around the fibres,

Spinning a deer hair body. When clipped to shape this will be a mottled sedge imitation.

pulling very gently as you ease the fibres evenly around the hook shank. Add two more turns and pull down slowly. The fibres will spin around the hook shank to create a chimney sweep's brush effect. Pull back the fibres and make three tight turns in front of the deer hair to secure the tying. Now you can add further pinches of hair in just the same way, building up a bushy body. If you use hair of varying shades, the final body will have a mottled effect – very useful when making artificial sedge flies. Finally, use sharp scissors to clip the deer hair to whatever shape you want. Muddlers, G & H Sedges, snail imitations and even small fry can be sculpted from spun deer hair.

4 Basic Techniques – Wings and Hackles

Some of the materials used for wings and hackles need special handling, and we will explain these as they arise in this chapter. Most of the tying techniques, however, are based upon the principles covered in Chapter 3. Therefore, when you have worked through Chapter 4 you will have the necessary skills to tie the majority of traditional and modern fly patterns.

WINGS

Dry fly wings are usually tied on before the hackles, whereas in many wet flies the hackle is fitted before the wing; but we have to start somewhere, so wings it will be.

For some reason winging has become known as the beginner's nightmare, but it need not be so. If you have mastered the

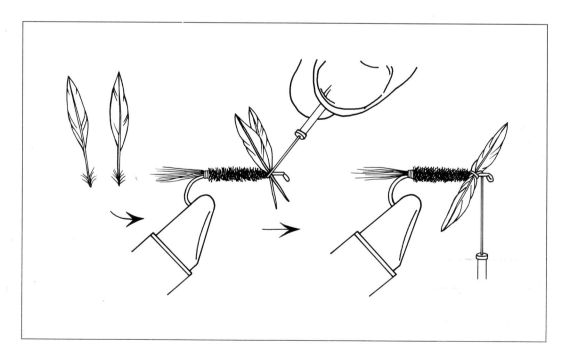

Fig 21   Tying hackle point spent wings.

pinch-and-loop method of attaching tails, then tying on wings is no more difficult. The only other problems you may encounter stem from poor preparation: it is essential to start with an accurately matched pair of feathers.

Hackle Point Wings

Spent (dead) mayflies, daddy-long-legs and damsel flies are three of the insects which can be copied using hackle points as wings.

After making the usual foundation layer, select a pair of matching cock hackles with short fibres. Strip off the soft flue and lower fibres to make two wings about the same length as the hook shank. Place the wings together, shiny side up, along the hook shank and lock the stalks in position with three pinch-and-loop turns. Make figure-of-eight turns with the tying thread to secure the wings in the spent position.

Feather Slip Wet Fly Wings

This is a widely used technique for winging wet flies. Take a pair of matching mallard feather slips – one from a right-wing feather, the other from the corresponding left-wing feather – and use your dubbing needle to pick out the same number of fibres for each slip. Put the two slips together, shiny sides outwards, and offer them up above the hook shank. Adjust the position until the wing tips just project beyond the bend of the hook. Use the pinch-and-loop technique, pulling down steadily whilst holding the wings in position. The feather fibres will compress

Tying Tip

To improve the durability of wings on sea trout flies, such as the Butcher, wipe the finished wing with a smear of varnish.

vertically. Repeat with two more turns to lock the wings tightly in place before trimming off the excess material.

Paired Dry Fly Wings

Dry fly wings are no more difficult to tie in than paired wet fly wings, except that smaller

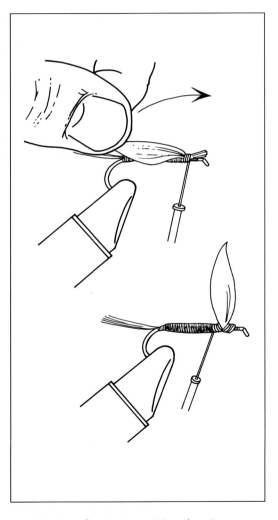

Fig 22   Dry fly winging: raising the wings to the vertical position.

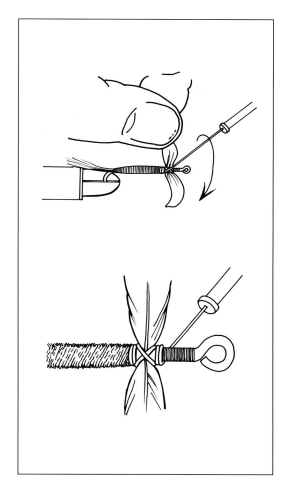

Fig 23 Dry fly wings: spreading the wings.

(leaving room for the head and two or three turns of hackle in front of the wings), hold the wing slips above the shank so that the tips reach just past the bend. Secure the wings with three pinch-and-loop turns before trimming off the excess wing material. Now take the tying thread behind the wings, making two full turns hard against the wing slips so the wings are forced into the vertical position.

The wings can be spread further apart, should you wish, by pulling down one wing at a time and taking the tying thread carefully between the wings, beneath the hook shank and up in front of the other wing. Repeat this process for the other wing so as to create two or three figure-of-eight turns. Finish off in front with the normal pinch-and-loop tying.

Streamer Wings

Various streamer and ghost lure patterns use paired cock hackle feathers as winging material. Select a pair of hackle points about one and a half times as long as your hook. Place the hackles back to back with the shiny side out, and offer them up above the body of the fly. Pull off the flue and lower fibres from the hackle stalks before locking the wing in place with three pinch-and-loop turns. If you wish, you can add a second pair of smaller wings or 'cheeks' – jungle cock feathers are used for this purpose on some fly patterns.

Matuka Wings

Prepare a fly body, leaving the ribbing wire or tinsel hanging free at the tail position. Prepare a pair of hackles as for normal streamer wings and then strip away the fibres from the lower half of the wing where it lies along the fly body. Tie in the hackle stalks in the usual way, with four or five tight turns of thread. Now grip the point of the hackles with one hand

hooks are generally used and you may want to adjust the angle of the wings to imitate various natural flies.

Prepare a hook with its foundation layer, and select a pair of wing slips from the primary wing feathers of a blackbird. This time hold them with the shiny sides together, and match them up so that the tips align. Now, with the tying thread about one and a half hook-eye diameters down the shank

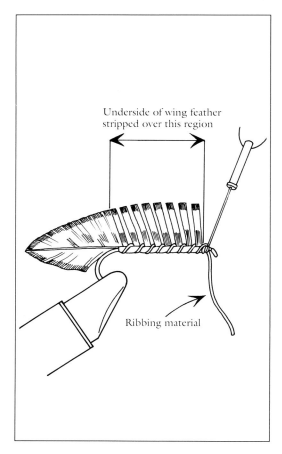

Underside of wing feather stripped over this region

Ribbing material

Fig 24 Fitting a matuka wing.

Hair Wings (Wet)

Hair wings have all but replaced feather wings in many salmon fishers' fly boxes. Hair is more durable, easier to tie and, with modern dyes, is available in a wide range of colours.

To tie a simple hair wing, prepare a hook with its foundation layer. Cut a bunch of calf tail hair and trim the butts (not the tips) so that the wing extends to just beyond the bend of the hook. With the butts against the eye of the hook, secure the wing with four pinch-and-loop turns. A touch of head varnish or superglue worked into the butts with the dubbing needle will ensure that the wing remains secure when the fly is in use. You can now add a neat head and whip finish, just to keep in practice.

Hair Wings (Dry)

One of the most popular of dry fly styles is represented in the Wulff series. This method of winging dry flies was devised by the late Lee Wulff, an American with an international reputation as an angler and innovative fly-tyer. His patterns have proven successful throughout. the world. Bucktail hair used in these dressings is both flexible and durable – a fly tyer's dream material.

Having wound your foundation layer as usual, bring the tying thread two-thirds of the way back towards the eye. Select a generous bunch of bucktail hair and tie it down with the points protruding two-thirds of a hook shank beyond the eye of the hook. Now pull back the hair tips, which will represent the wings, and wind six turns of tying thread hard against the bucktail to raise the wing into a near-vertical position. Take the thread half-way down the body trapping the hair as you go. Trim off the hair and secure with tying thread before bringing the thread back to the head position.

and stroke the hackle fibres forward with the other hand until they sit vertically.

Now for the ribbing! Make one full turn with the ribbing material at the end of the fly body, thus trapping the hackle points. Next, wind the ribbing in five even turns up along the body, parting the wing fibres as you go. The wing could now represent the spined dorsal of a perch fry, for example. Lock in the end of the ribbing material, add the hackle and head, and you have a matuka lure.

Whiskey: a streamer fly with added cheek feathers.

A matuka lure.

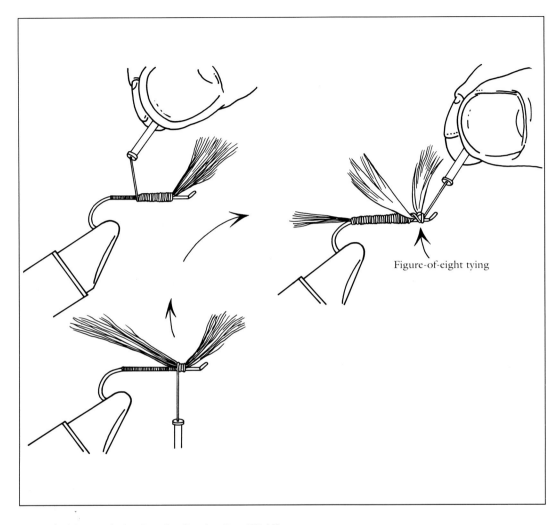

Figure-of-eight tying

Fig 25 Tying a hair wing dry fly: the Grey Wulff.

Tying Tip

Tie in the hair so you work from the body towards the eye of the hook. Pull up the ends at right angles to the hook before cutting them off; this gives a neat, tapering finish.

To split the wing, divide the hair into two equal bunches, then run three or four figure-of-eight turns of the tying thread between the wings.

This style of winging provides a realistic representation of a hovering stonefly or upwinged fly alighting to deposit eggs onto the surface.

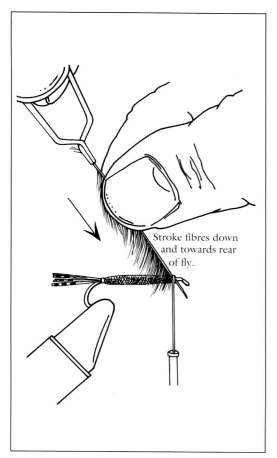

Fig 26 Spider patterns use soft hen hackles which can be folded double before tying in.

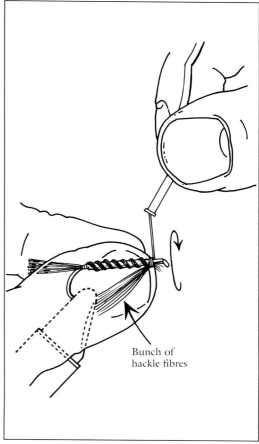

Fig 27 A 'false' beard hackle is an alternative to a full collar hackle drawn down at the throat of the fly.

HACKLES

The term hackle has several meanings to fly tyers. One use of a hackle is to represent the legs of an insect. Although all insects have just six legs, trout will accept flies with many more, and this helps us make dry flies which float on the surface despite the presence within them of a steel hook. (Most dry flies will sink once pushed through the surface film; it is only surface tension which keeps them afloat.)

In wet flies, we can use a throat hackle to represent the pectoral fins of a small fish. The success of such patterns as Bloody Butcher may well rely on this aspect of imitation. Hackle is also the name given to the neck feathers of a game bird, so perhaps it is

Hair wing wet and dry flies. Top row: Blue Charm. Middle row: Garry, Whiskey.
Bottom row: Grey Wulff, Royal Wulff.

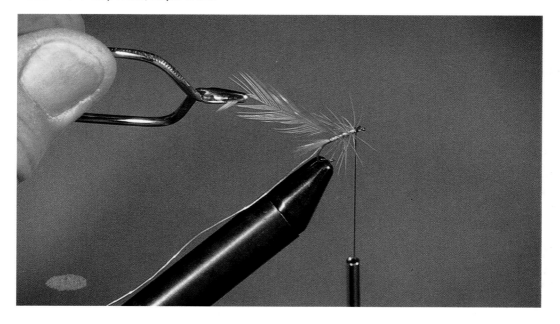

Palmering a bob fly – the Wickham's Fancy.

Feathers: the raw materials for wings and hackles. The dull feathers are more useful when imitating insects, while bright, dyed feathers will often incite a trout to seize a lure.

Capes: the source of hackle feathers. There is a tremendous variety of colours available in natural capes like these, while dyed capes extend the range still further.

fortunate that we use these feathers more often than not when tying the hackle of an artificial fly.

Collar Hackles

Having completed the foundation layer, return the tying thread back to just behind the head position. Now choose a cock hackle whose fibres are one and a half times the hook gape. Strip away the soft downy flue and lower fibres. Lock in the hackle at the stalk end with three pinch-and-loop turns. Grip the hackle tip with your pliers and pull it through 180 degrees over the eye of the hook, ensuring that the shiny side is towards the eye. Now raise the hackle away from the hook shank and wind on four close turns, keeping the hackle at right angles to the hook shank. Next, wind the tying thread carefully through the hackle without trapping any of the fibres. Lock in the hackle tip with three pinch-and-loop turns before trimming off the excess. This is your dry fly hackle, all ready for the head and whip finish.

Wet fly collar hackles, as used in spider patterns, for example, can be tied in much the same way, but you will want a more streamlined shape, so the hackle should be raked backwards. We normally use soft hen hackles for wet flies, as they absorb water more quickly and are much softer than cock hackles, and so the fly sinks more readily and is more lively in the water. (With large wet flies and lures, the heavy hook usually determines the rate of sinking, so the more durable cock hackles can be used.) When you have wound the hackle, make three or four tight turns of tying thread hard against the front of the hackle. This will slope the hackles towards the tail of the fly.

An alternative method for wet fly hackles involves folding the hackle feather down the middle before winding on the hackle. This technique works best with very soft hen hackles.

Beard or Throat Hackles

Many wet fly patterns require hackles underneath the head, rather than all round. You could, of course, tie a collar hackle, pulling it down under the hook shank before you add the wings and head; however, this does give a rather bulky result.

An alternative approach is to use a false hackle. Simply peel off a bunch of fibres from the side of a hackle feather and hold them beneath the hook at the throat position. The hackle tips should be just long enough to reach to the hook point. Secure with two pinch-and-loop turns and your fly is ready for the wings and head.

Palmering

When a hackle feather is wound along the whole length of the body of a dry fly, we call it a palmered pattern. These extremely buoyant lake flies are often used for dapping – fishing a fly so that the wind makes it bob along on the tops of the waves.

Start with a silk floss body and with a gold wire at the bend ready for ribbing. Do not rib the body yet. Tie in at the head a cock hackle whose longest fibres are twice the hook gape. Wind the first two turns of hackle close together. Now continue winding back towards the bend of the hook with neatly spaced turns of hackle. Use a single turn of the ribbing wire to tie down the end of the hackle, and then continue the ribbing along the body, working it between the fibres so that none of the fibres become trapped. Finally tie off the ribbing and trim away the surplus hackle stalk. You are now ready to add a head and a whip finish to complete your palmered bob fly.

TABLE 4-1

Component	Common Tying Faults
foundation layer	incomplete or not securely wound, so the fly body can rotate around the hook shank
tail	too long – tied in too far round the bend of the hook not correctly positioned on top of hook shank
body	too bulky
hackle wing	too long for the size of the hook being used loosely spread out instead of closely wound turns too short or too long not directly on top of the hook shank not accurately paired, so the wing sweeps to the left or right
head	too large tied too far forward, obscuring the eye of the hook tied too far back, leaving a bare hook shank around the eye

COMMON TYING FAULTS

We have already said that fly proportions vary considerably, so what is right for one pattern could be wrong for another. However, in the table above we list some of the most common tying mistakes, so you are forewarned!

If you can tie each of the component parts of a fly without suffering the problems listed above, you have fully mastered the basic skills of fly tying. Now you can progress with confidence to the serious business of stocking your fly box, at the same time learning a range of advanced tips and techniques.

5 Natural and Artificial Flies

Before moving on from basic tying skills to the techniques for tying a range of flies, it is worth considering what we are trying to achieve. In fishing, there is little room for the words always and never; this applies equally to fly tying. Techniques which improve the attractiveness of one pattern may detract from another. For example, while lengthening the tail may make a marabou lure more enticing to a rainbow trout in spring, it could result in short takes and lost fish when summer sea trout are your quarry. Much depends on what prompts the fish to seize the fly.

WHY DO FISH TAKE ARTIFICIAL FLIES?

Perhaps the most obvious answer is that the trout mistakes our artificial fly for food of some sort. But how closely does a trout inspect what it eats? That, surely, is a crucial consideration for fly tyers. The answer is: 'It all depends. . .' Below are three situations in which a feeding trout might be deceived:

1   The fly is about the same size as a 'food' creature, and it is in a position where the fish has got used to finding food. So, without bothering to inspect it closely, the fish swallows the fly.
2   Upon cursory inspection, the trout sees something that is a similar size and shape to, and is behaving like, a creature on which it has been feeding. The unsuspecting fish therefore eats the fly.
3   Even after careful inspection, the trout decides that the offering looks and behaves very much like a creature upon which it feeds; so, any fears allayed, the fish proceeds to eat the fly.

Clearly the accuracy of your imitation and the amount of skill necessary in fishing it must be much greater in case 3 than in case 1.

So far we have only considered ways of catching the actively feeding fish. Salmon and sea trout spend most of their time in the river without seeking food, yet they too can be caught by fly fishers. Below are three more reasons why a fish might take a fly, and we think these are applicable to both migratory and non-migratory fish:

1   The fly resembles an injured creature, inciting the bullying instinct in the fish.
2   The fly annoys the fish, perhaps by encroaching into its territory, so the fish reacts by striking out with its only weapon – its mouth.
3   The behaviour of the fly arouses curiosity in the fish, which investigates the fly using the only tool available to it – its mouth.

Compare a fly catalogue with any book on entomology and you may well decide that

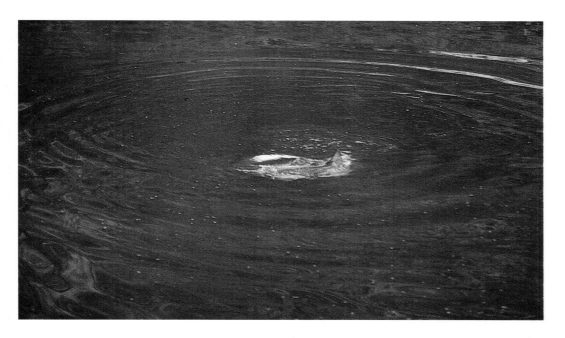

Deception complete: a rainbow trout rises to a dry fly.

Salmon flies: no insect representations here.

salmon fly patterns are either fish imitations or simply something intended to arouse curiosity or annoyance in the quarry.

At times the quality of imitation can be extremely important, for example when fishing for wild trout whose usual source of food is natural insect life; while durability – the result of skilful tying of quality materials on to quality hooks – matters most when fishing freshly stocked waters or when migratory fish are your quarry.

When Do You Need a Close Imitation?

Provided they have no reason to fear danger from a predator, trout in wild places are usually the most gullible, snatching at food without a moment's hesitation. However, trout soon become more cautious on heavily fished waters, where they are inclined to give a fly much more than a cursory glance before accepting it; they can also become very choosy when an abundance of food is available. This supports our findings that, while behaviour of the artificial fly is important, it is rarely good enough simply to tie on any old pattern. Indeed there are many occasions when the pattern of the fly is second only to the cunning of the angler (caution in approach, care in concealment and good presentation) in determining success or failure.

All this favours the fly fisher who is not restricted to the limited selection of patterns and sizes stocked by the local tackle shop. But there is more to it than that. Rainbow trout most often move about in shoals, and it seems that on some of the most popular stillwaters the shoals get to recognize certain patterns of lures. These patterns which once were so successful are now being fished by all and sundry; the trout get to know them and, we suspect, to see them as danger signals. If you come along with an interesting little design of

your own, however, you may well overcome that innate cautiousness and trigger the predatory reaction.

CLASSIFICATION OF ARTIFICIAL FLIES

It remains something of a mystery why some designs take fish consistently while other patterns, including many which appear to us as better imitations of real food creatures, are more often than not rejected by the quarry. Some successful patterns are close imitations of specific species, and it is easy to understand trout taking them in mistake for their favourite snack. But other so-called 'fancy' patterns continue to take trout which are feeding on flies of quite different size, shape or colour. Another group of artificial flies are neither close imitations of one insect species nor even general representations of a group of species of food creatures, but rather they fall into the category of attractor flies or lures, many of which are unlike anything living on this planet.

No doubt many of these strange concoctions provoke aggression on the part of the trout. We also suspect that some lures are taken as food – in much the same way as we are prepared to taste food we have not tried before (provided it looks appetizing). Apart from the obvious factors of its visibility and the way it swims through the water, most aspects of lure design are matters of trial and error. This would explain why some popular lures are equally effective when tied in a range of colour combinations.

What Makes a Successful Lure?

Lures do not have to imitate specific living creatures, so fly tyers can, and do, experiment with materials and colours. Yet only a minority of designs stand the test of time, tempting trout consistently with their combinations of colour, shape and movement through the water. Why is this, and what does trigger a trout into taking a lure? Some clues may come from considering one or two successful patterns.

Take the Sweeney Todd, for example. We believe the red throat and the barred silver-and-black body make this a fish imitator – it could be mistaken for a cock stickleback sporting its mating colours. But this does not explain the success of the Sweeney Todd on

waters which hold no sticklebacks; so it seems more likely that the red throat triggers the trout into seizing what it sees to be an injured and bleeding fish. Therefore it will come as no surprise to find that red features in a great many successful lure patterns.

A very effective lure which has no red in it at all is the Viva. The fluorescent green tail seems to be an important trigger point, begging the question: is red-green colour-blindness as common in trout as it is in male human beings? We wonder whether the Viva catches more cock fish than hen fish?

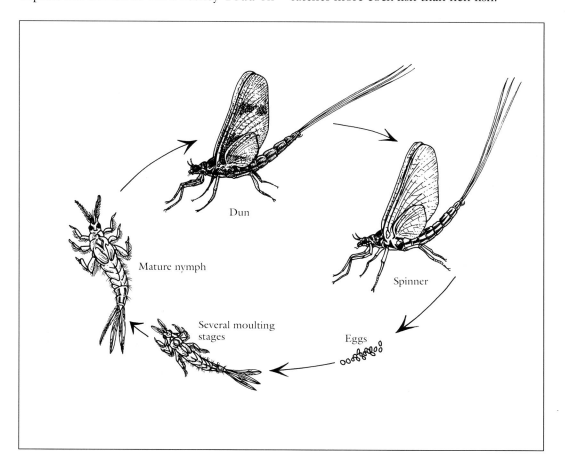

Dun

Mature nymph

Several moulting stages

Spinner

Eggs

Fig 28   Life-cycle of an upwinged fly, from egg, nymph and dun to egg-laying spinner.

Categories of trout flies: lure (Viva), general representation (Kite's Imperial), and close imitation (Sherry Spinner).

An upwinged fly, the Blue Winged Olive (Sherry) Spinner.

There is another very important feature of the Viva, however, which, we feel, contributes greatly to its effectiveness, and that is the way it moves when it is in the water. The marabou plume wing undulates as the fly is retrieved jerkily, giving the impression of a disabled creature incapable of swimming smoothly.

Therefore, when designing your own lures, try building in trigger points such as a red tail or throat and using materials which will pulsate as the fly moves through the water. There is still a great deal of scope for creativity in this area.

Matching the Hatch

Imitative fly design places rather more emphasis on colour matching. We should be aware, however, that the range or spectrum of light waves to which a trout's eye is sensitive differs somewhat from the spectral sensitivity of the human eye. Silk or fur which to us appears a perfect match for the body of a particular fly may not look so convincing to a trout.

The message, surely, is clear: by all means experiment with fly-tying materials until you are satisfied with the durability and

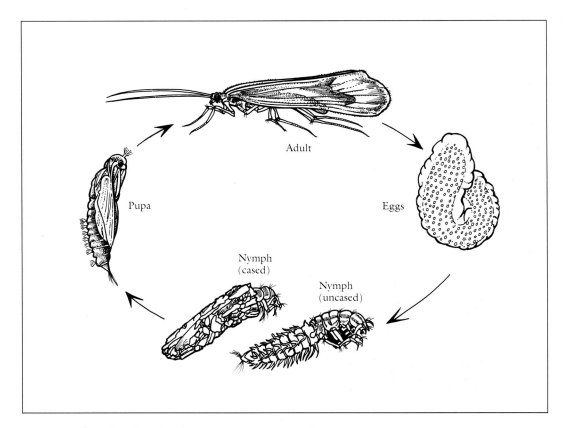

Fig 29 Life-cycle of a sedge fly.

appearance of your fly. Then let it have a very thorough testing by the most critical of judges, your quarry.

This chapter closes by showing the links between entomologists' terms for the insects they study and fly tiers' names for the various parts of an artificial fly.

Fig 28 shows the life cycle of a natural fly of the upwinged or Ephemeroptera order. This order includes the familiar mayfly and many smaller flies to be found on both rivers and lakes.

Sedge flies of the order Tricoptera are important throughout the season. They vary considerably in size, but are remarkably consistent in shape and – apart from a few mavericks – colour too. A limited number of patterns therefore will serve as imitations of sedge larvae, pupae and adult winged flies. The sedge fly life cycle is illustrated in Fig 29.

In Fig 30 a stonefly nymph and an adult fly, of the order Plecoptera, are illustrated. Stoneflies are very important during cold weather, particularly on rivers and streams in Scotland and the north of England. As trout are rarely selective in their feeding when stoneflies are hatching, the small differences between species are rarely given special attention by fly tyers. Instead we use just one or two general representations. The stonefly artificial is relatively simple compared with the mayfly artificial.

On lakes and slow-flowing rivers the midges or Chironomidae, those annoying biting insects of the river bank, are vital summer food sources for trout. Fig 30 shows the life cycle of these tiny flies. For the stillwater angler a hatch of midges or 'buzzers' can signal spectacular fishing during the evening rise, provided the right pattern of larva or winged insect acceptable to the trout can be found.

Many other creatures, both aquatic and

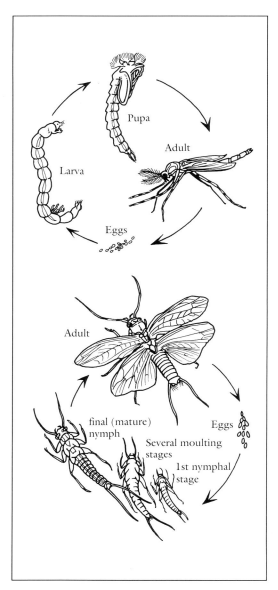

Fig 30 Life-cycle of the midge or chironomid (top) and the stonefly (bottom).

terrestrial, feature in the diets of trout and other feeding game fish. Most of these have artificial flies to match them and in the

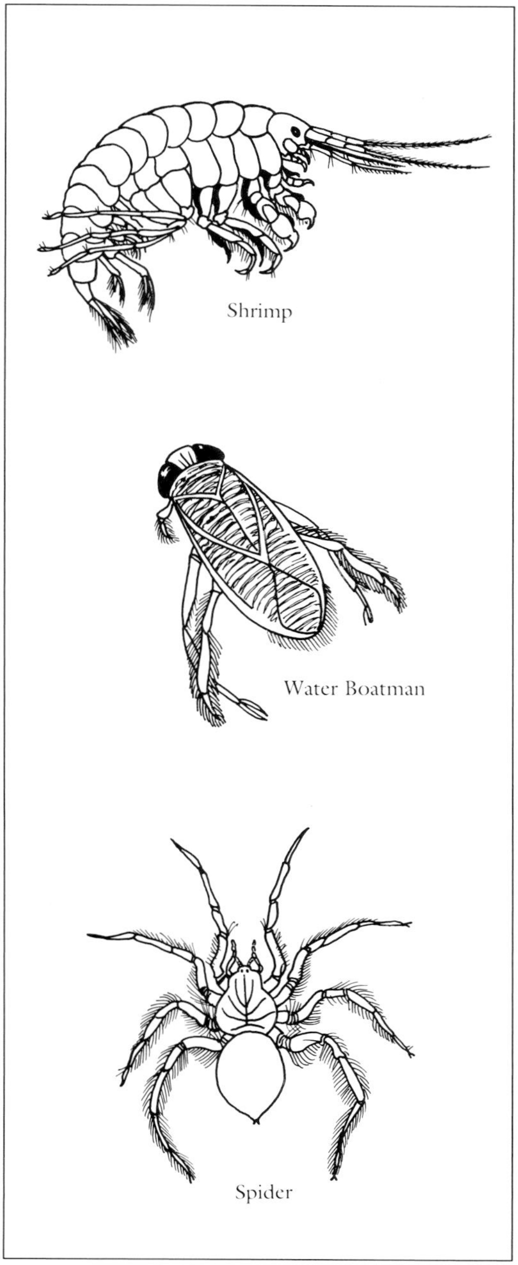

Shrimp

Water Boatman

Spider

Fig 31 Shrimp, spider and water boatman, three other items in the trout's diet.

chapters that follow we will show how to tie a good selection of them.

The Scope for Creativity

There are millions of insects in the world, the majority of which live in or around water, so fly tyers are unlikely to run out of opportunities to develop new imitations for many years to come. But why limit yourself to flies? The trout certainly don't!

Just consider the variety of beetles you find by rivers and lakes, for example. All of these can get blown on to the water from time to time, and if you are there at the time with a credible imitation of one of these beetles, your luck could be in.

But remember, it's not just the winged adults that trout feed upon. Indeed, as far as beetles are concerned, many have aquatic larvae which look and behave rather like nymphs, although they are far more voracious. (Beetle larvae feed on small fishes; the survivors no doubt get their own back later!)

Subjects for Study

If you decide to develop your own imitations, here's an important lesson we had to learn the hard way: don't work from pictures in books. Line illustrations are often misleading, and some bear little resemblance to the insects. (Keith Linsell, who illustrated this book, has first-hand knowledge of water life; sadly, some illustrators are less professional in their approach.)

Even photographs are a poor guide to colour, partly because colour reproduction is rarely faithful to the original, but partly too because the lighting conditions alter the appearance of insects. So, try to collect live samples and study them in varying light levels

A Mayfly Spinner. The wings reflect whatever colour light is shone upon them, so artificial flies with blue, black or orange wings are all successful at various times of the day.

and at different times of the day. Then you can tie artificial flies to match the insect in a particular situation.

For example, we always exaggerate the brightness of the orange body of the Sherry spinner, because when you are fishing at dusk it is this part of the fly which best reflects the evening light.

6 Shrimps, Nymphs and Pupae

Bearing in mind that trout obtain most of their food below the surface, and that for most of the day there may be little or no sign of insect hatches, we surely must reduce our chances of success if we insist on always fishing on or in the surface layer. Therefore, important questions must be: how well do the trout see their food deep below the surface, and how good must our imitations be? The answer, as you might expect, is that it all depends...

In turbulence or in muddy water the trout get a hazy view of insects swimming or drifting nearby. For these situations you can often get away with crude general representations. But there will be many other times

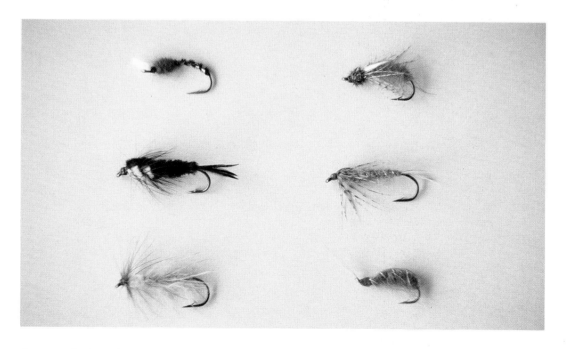

A range of sub-surface food imitators. Top row: Buzzer, Sedge Pupa. Middle row: Montana Nymph, Damsel Nymph. Bottom row: Cased Caddis, Shrimp.

AN INTRODUCTION TO FLY TYING

when you will need close copies of the particular creatures on which the trout are feeding; anything else may be steadfastly ignored. From this chapter you will learn how to tie shrimps, sedge pupae and buzzers which bear scrutiny by the most fastidious of fickle feeders. You will be able to use these patterns with even greater confidence, of course, as general representations when the trout are really on a binge. We have also included a modern nymph which will serve as a general representation for stillwater fishing.

A WEIGHTED FLY – THE LEADED SHRIMP

Most rivers and streams, and many gravelly lakes, have large populations of freshwater shrimps. Trout love them! This pattern is heavily weighted to sink to the bed where it can be fished using the sink-and-draw technique by retrieving a few inches of (floating) fly line, pausing for a second or two, then retrieving again.

Materials

Hook	Sedge hook size 10 (10 to 14).
Tying thread	Red.
Underbody	Lead strip.
Body	A blend of olive and 'hot orange' seal fur.
Feelers	Olive cock hackle fibres.
Rib	Gold oval tinsel.
Back	Stretched polythene.

Tying Details

Begin by preparing the materials. Cut up a strong clear polythene bag into strips ¼in. wide. Stretch the polythene until it shrinks to about half its original width – you will be able

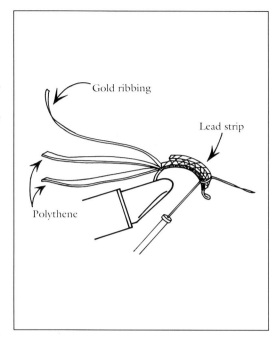

Fig 32 Leaded Shrimp: adding lead to the hook.

to feel when all the stretch has gone out of the polythene. This will form the shell-like back of the shrimp. Now cut a 4in length of lead foil about ⅟₁₆in. wide. (The heavy foil from the tops of wine bottles is equally suitable.)

For this weighted shrimp you will need to bring the foundation layer well round the bend of the hook. Tie in the polythene at its

Tying Tip

Make each layer of lead foil shorter than the preceding one. This will give your shrimp a realistic humped back, and will also reduce the chances of the point of the hook snagging on the bed of the river or lake when you are retrieving the shrimp.

60

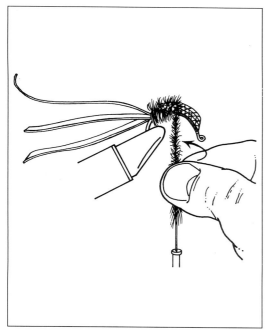

Fig 33 Leaded Shrimp: dubbing the body.

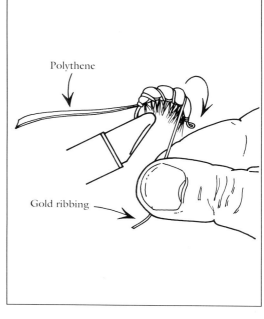

Fig 34 Leaded Shrimp: ribbing the under-layer of polythene.

central point, folding both ends back over the bend of the hook for the time being. Tie in the gold ribbing, and you are ready to add the lead.

Tie in the lead strip at the middle of the hook bend, laying it forward along the top of the hook and binding it down to a point ³⁄₁₆in. behind the eye of the hook. Fold back the lead and continue binding it down to a position above the hook bend. Repeat this process with two more layers of lead.

Blend 75 per cent olive-green with 25 hot orange seal fur (or substitute) by rubbing the fibres together in a circular motion in the palm of your hand. Dub on the seal fur over the entire body. Tie in the feelers facing forwards over the eye of the hook, and trim off any spare butts. You are now ready to add a shell back to your shrimp.

Stroke the dubbing fibres backwards as you fold the first strip of polythene over the back of the shrimp. Pull the polythene tight and lock it down securely at the head position using the tying thread. Wind a rib with five turns of the tinsel on top of the polythene and tie off at the head. Now tie in six olive cock hackle fibres, facing forwards over the eye of the hook; they will represent the shrimp's feelers.

You can now fold the second layer of polythene over the back of the shrimp and tie it in at the head. Notice how the ribbing shows through, giving a most realistic imitation of the segmented body of the natural shrimp.

To complete the shrimp, wind a small neat head, whip finish, and apply two coats of clear varnish.

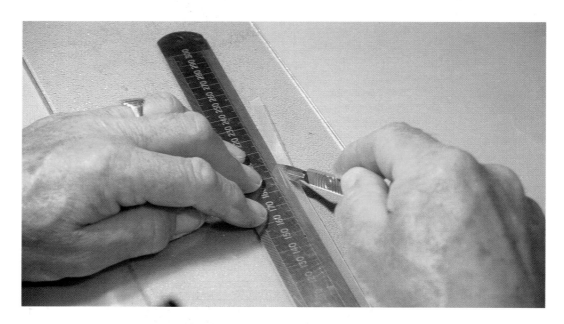

Leaded Shrimp: preparing the polythene strips.

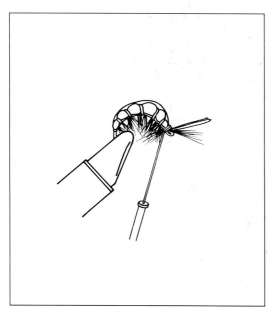

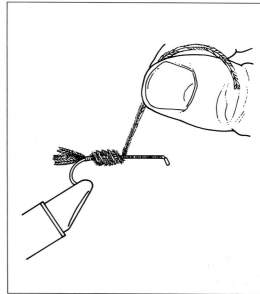

Fig 35 Leaded Shrimp: tying down the final layer of polythene.

Fig 36 Montana Nymph: tying in the black chenille abdomen.

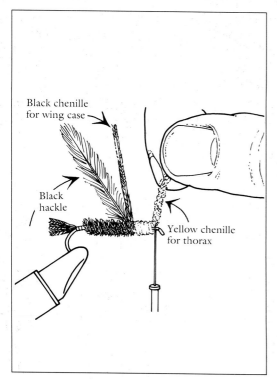

Fig 37 Montana Nymph: adding the yellow chenille thorax.

Fig 38 Montana Nymph: winding in the hackle.

CHENILLE PATTERN – MONTANA NYMPH

The Montana Nymph is used as a general representation of large nymphs on stillwaters, where it is a reasonable imitator of the dragonfly nymph. This American pattern uses both black and yellow chenille, a superb material for rapidly building up bulky bodies.

Materials

Hook	Size 10 long shank (8 and 10).

Tying thread	Black.
Tail	Three black cock hackle tips tied as a 'trident'.
Body	Black chenille.
Thorax	Yellow chenille.
Hackle	Black cock.
Wing case	Black chenille.

Tying Details

Having wound a foundation layer, tie in the hackle tip tails. Prepare the black chenille by stripping off the flue from the last ⅛in. Tie in the centre core of the chenille and wind a body in tight turns to the thorax position. Tie down the black chenille and fold back the spare end above the top of the hook shank. Strip the flue from ⅛in of the yellow chenille and tie it in. Now catch in a black cock hackle before running the tying thread forward to the head position and tying it down.

Tying Tip

Carefully stroke the hackle backwards as you bring the free end of the black chenille forward to represent the wing case. This will help avoid hackle fibres becoming trapped, and will ensure you end up with a symmetrical nymph which swims correctly.

Now for the thorax, legs and wing case. Three or four turns of the yellow chenille should take you to the head position, where

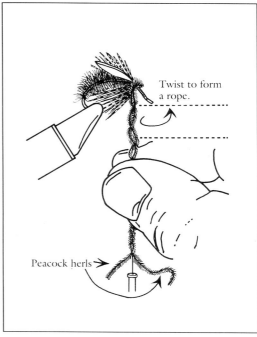

Fig 40   Sedge Pupa: adding a peacock herl head.

you will need to tie down the chenille. Next, wind three turns of the hackle over the thorax and tie it down at the head position.

Trap the black chenille securely with the tying thread, trim off all the excess materials, and you are ready to wind the head. A coat of varnish to finish and behold, the Montana Nymph!

EMERGER – SEDGE PUPA

Having risen to the surface, many species of sedge flies take quite some time to wriggle free from their pupal shucks. Struggling in the surface film, they attract the attention of the trout which seize them, often with great swirling rises, as they attempt to get airborne

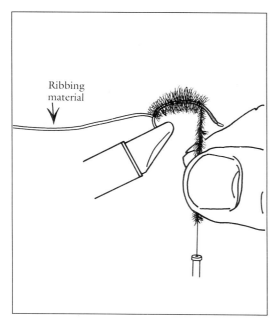

Fig 39   Sedge Pupa: dubbing the body.

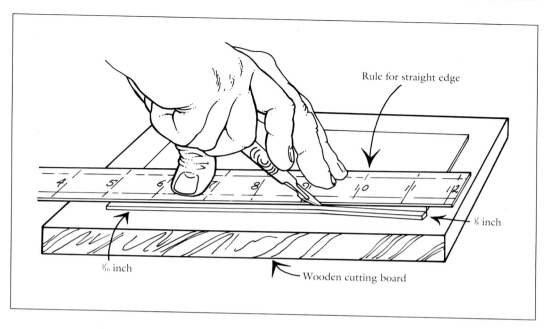

Rule for straight edge

⅛ inch

1/16 inch

Wooden cutting board

Fig 41   Black Buzzer: preparing the ethafoam.

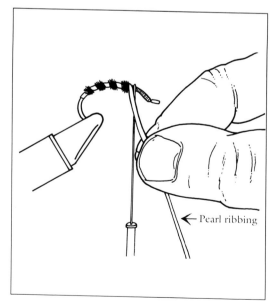

← Pearl ribbing

Fig 42   Black Buzzer: ribbing the abdomen.

on that vital maiden voyage. Fished just under the surface in the late evening rise, this pattern represents the emerging sedge fly.

Materials

Hook	Sedge hook size 10 (10 to 14).
Tying thread	Black.
Body	Hot orange seal fur.
Rib	Firebrand fluorescent orange.
Emerging wings	Grey goose biots.
Hackle	Light partridge.
Head	Peacock herl.

Tying Details

After making the foundation layer, tie in the fluorescent orange ribbing material and then dub a seal fur body to within ³⁄₁₆in of the eye.

65

Leaded Shrimp: the finished fly. Note how the body segments show through the polythene 'shell' back.

Montana Nymph: the finished fly.

Sedge Pupa: the finished fly.

Black Buzzer: the finished fly.

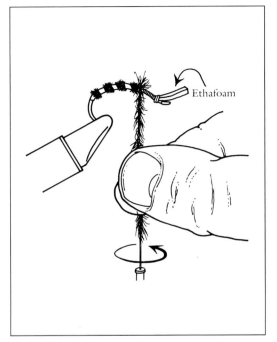

Fig 43   Black Buzzer: dubbing the thorax.

Fig 44   Black Buzzer: shaping the ethafoam

Add two goose biots angled up and back to represent the emerging wings. Next tie in the hackle feather and make just two turns to represent legs.

The large head of the sedge is simulated in peacock herl. Tie in two herls and twist them with tying thread to form a rope. Form the head of the pupa with three close turns of the peacock herl rope. Tie down, add a neat whip finish and secure with varnish.

ETHAFOAM SUSPENDER PATTERN – BLACK BUZZER

This is another emerger pattern, representing a chironomid just before it hatches into the familiar buzzing midge. The buzzer pupa sits

right at the surface, and on really calm evenings it can take quite some time to break through the surface film. This artificial pupa is effective when fished stationary or on a very slow, twitching retrieve. It is a great fly for the evening rise in high summer.

Materials

Hook	Sedge hook size 12 (10 to 16).
Tying thread	Black.
Body	Black condor herl or substitute.
Rib	Pearl tinsel.
Thorax	Natural mole fur.
Breathing filaments	White ethafoam.

Tying Details

First prepare the ethafoam by cutting it into strips ⅛in. wide and ⅟₁₆in. thick. You will only need a ¼in. length of ethafoam strip for each buzzer, but, if you are tying several in a batch, do not cut it into short pieces. Instead, leave the foam in a long strip as it will be easier to handle and you will waste less.

Tying Tip

Shape the ethafoam breathing filaments after tying the rest of the buzzer pupa. Use sharp scissors to snip the ethafoam along the centre line; it will part neatly to form a 'V'. Trim the corners of the ethafoam to produce triangular tips to the breathing filaments. The buzzer will float with these tips just breaking the surface.

Run the foundation thread from head to bend, and tie in the condor herl and the pearl rib. Bring the tying thread forward to the thorax position. Wind the body herl in close turns to the thorax position and lock it down. Wind on the body rib and tie it down, running the thread forward to the eye.

Now to create the breathing filaments and the thorax. Tie in the ethafoam and pull or cut off the excess. Take the tying thread back to the thorax position. Dub on the mole fur, winding it forward to form a humped thorax. Finally, make a neat whip finish and varnish.

BUZZER VARIATIONS

As chironomid pupae are so important to stillwater anglers, and are now finding growing acceptance by dedicated stream fishers too, it's worth mentioning the wealth of opportunity these tiny insects offer to the innovative fly tyer.

For the breathing filaments, you can choose from a variety of man-made fibres, including the inner core from the mylar tubing. Feather herl is another obvious material to try, and one of the best of these is marabou, which wafts enticingly in the slightest current.

Buzzer Body Colours

For the body, try various feather herls, fine wools and even plastics, in a range of natural colours including black as well as various greens and browns.

Brown bodied buzzers are an excellent match for the pupa of the Phantom Fly, which sometimes hatches in large numbers from pools and lakes in early summer.

A buzzer pattern with tremendous scope for variation uses pre-stretched nylon monofilament. This material is available in a good range of colours including browns, greens and blues. This pattern was devised by Bob Carnill.

A completed Carnill Buzzer is shown overleaf. The materials used in this pattern are as follows:

Materials

Hook	Size 12 Yorkshire Sedge (Partridge K2B)
Tying Thread	Black
Body	Pre-stretched nylon monofilament
Thorax	Dubbed mole fur
Filaments	White marabou

A Carnill Buzzer. The nylon monofilament body gives tremendous scope for matching the hatch.

Reward for a successfully tied fly used at the right time.

7 Wet Flies

Wet flies have a history stretching back to the beginning of angling writing and, no doubt, beyond. Long scorned by chalk-stream purists, wet fly techniques are seen by spate river and lake anglers as a most valuable element in their strategy. Indeed, spring and autumn would be bleak times if fly fishers were restricted to floating flies when the trout are chasing fry in a reservoir or scavenging on the bed of a swollen river.

There is some argument as to what traditional wet flies actually represent. Some certainly look rather like hatching insects – the Mallard and Claret is an example – while other, brighter patterns such as Teal, Blue and Silver, are more likely taken as fish. The view is sometimes expressed that wet flies are crude and unselective; they can be, particularly when fished so that they swim against a strong current – something that nymphs and drowning flies cannot do. That such fishing methods take trout cannot be denied. This argument is countered by the many wet fly experts who say these types of flies should be fished by casting upstream and across the current, so they behave like drowning insects struggling desperately against impossible odds.

Whatever they represent, wet flies are certainly worth having with you when you go fishing on lakes or rough streams. The patterns described below make use of a range of furs and feathers, and we have included tying tips to help you handle these materials more easily.

A PALMERED WET FLY – INVICTA

Invented by James Ogden in 1879, the Invicta is an excellent lake fly. When it is fished just under the surface, trout probably take it as a hatching sedge fly. In size 14 the Invicta serves as an effective imitation of the grannom, a welcome offering to spate river brown trout in the opening weeks of the season.

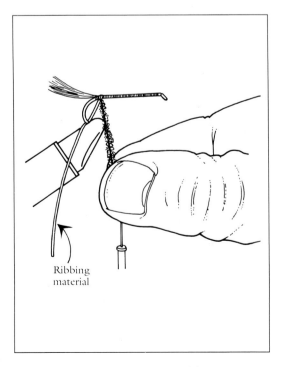

Ribbing material

Fig 45   Invicta: dubbing the seal fur.

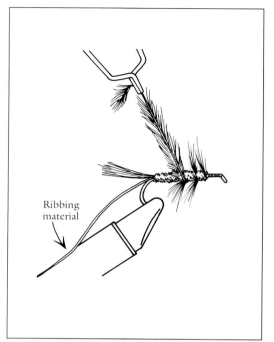

Fig 46   Invicta: palmering the body.

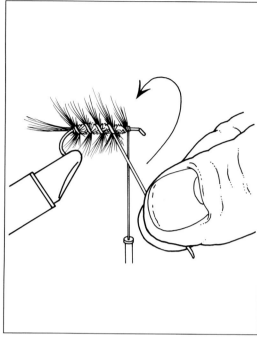

Fig 47   Invicta: winding the wire rib.

Materials

Hook	Down-eye size 10 (8 to 14).
Tying thread	Black.
Tail	Golden pheasant topping (crest) feather.
Body	Yellow seal fur or substitute.
Body hackle	Light-red palmered cock hackle.
Rib	Oval gold tinsel.
Wings	Hen pheasant centre tail feather.
Throat hackle	Dyed blue guinea-fowl (Gallena).

Tying Details

After making a foundation, tie in a single golden pheasant topping (crest) feather and then the tinsel rib at the bend of the hook. Dub yellow seal fur on to the thread and wind a dubbed body.

Now for the palmering. Tie in a light-red cock hackle and wind six turns in a regular spiral back to the tail position. Use the tinsel rib to secure the end of the body hackle, and then rib the body, tying the tinsel down at the head position.

Trim off any spare body hackle and ribbing materials before adding a false beard hackle of dyed guinea-fowl. If you fail to spot "Guinea-fowl" feathers when searching

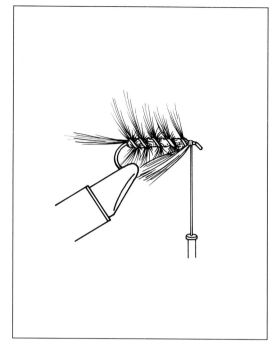

Fig 48   Invicta: adding the throat hackle.

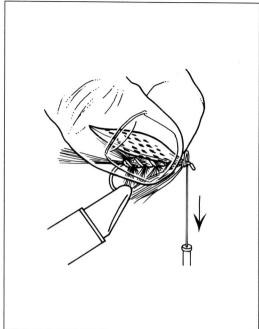

Fig 49   Invicta: tying in the wings.

Tying Tip
To create surface disturbance when fishing late at night, use a pair of body hackles wound together to create a bushy fly.

through a mail order catalogue, try looking for their alternative name which is 'Gallena'.

For the wings, prepare matched feather slips from either side of a hen pheasant centre tail feather. (You do not need a matching pair of feathers, of course.) Tie in the wings using the pinch-and-loop technique. Wind a small, neat head, whip finish to secure the tying and varnish the head.

A TINSEL-BODIED FLY – BUTCHER

A great sea trout fly especially when fished in quiet pools at night, for over 150 years the Butcher has also been a popular trout fly on river and stream. In clear water it is best worked slowly through quiet pools for sea trout, or just sub-surface in gentle glides for wild brown trout. As a lake fly it is often fished as the point fly in a team of three or more. The Bloody Butcher, with its scarlet throat hackle, is a very good fly for the middle dropper and is often fished with a bushy bob fly on the top dropper.

Use hook sizes 6 to 12 for seatrout fishing, while hook sizes 10 to 16 should be used for both river and stillwater trout fishing.

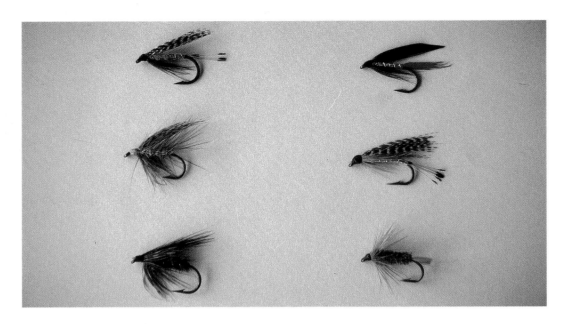

A range of wet flies for trout and grayling. Top row: Peter Ross, Butcher. Middle row: Invicta, Teal, Blue & Silver. Bottom row: Connemara Black, Red Tag.

Invicta: the finished fly.

Butcher: the finished fly.

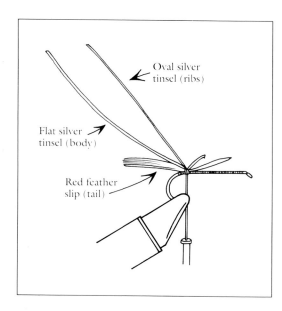

Fig 50 Butcher: tying in tail and body materials.

Materials

Hook	Down-eye size 10 (6 to 16).
Tying thread	Black.
Tail	Red ibis or substitute (dyed goose wing).
Body	Silver flat tinsel.
Rib	Silver oval tinsel.
Wings	Blue mallard wing.
Throat hackle	Black cock.

Tying Details

After fitting the foundation layer, tie in the tail material and a length of oval tinsel. Take the thread back to the head position, where you should tie in a length of flat silver tinsel. Wind the flat tinsel in neat overlapping turns down to the bend of the hook and back again to the head position to form the body. Rib

75

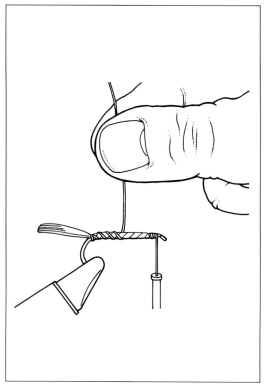

Fig 51   Butcher: ribbing the tinsel body.

Fig 52   Butcher: tying in the wings.

the body with the oval tinsel and secure at the head. Trim off any waste tinsel.

Tying Tip

When tying the Butcher for fishing sea trout, use heavy-gauge metal tinsel for improved durability: the teeth of a large sea trout make short work of silver mylar. Keep the tail very short: this reduces the chance of missing takes from lazy summer sea trout which tend to nip the tail of the fly.

Fit a false beard hackle beneath the head, using cock hackle fibres which just reach to the point of the hook. Finally, select a matching pair of blue-black mallard wing slips and tie them in; add a neat head and finish the fly in the usual way.

HAIR-WINGED SALMON FLY – A BLUE CHARM

Originally tied using a wing built up from mallard, teal and golden pheasant topping feathers, this hair wing version has lost none of the attraction of the original. A dull pattern

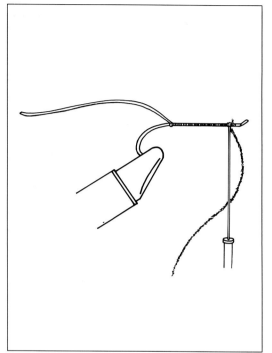

Fig 53 Blue Charm: tinsel and floss tied in ready to make the body.

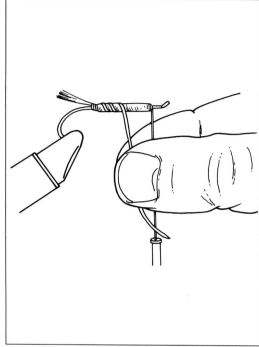

Fig 54 Blue Charm: ribbing the body.

by traditional salmon fly standards, the Blue Charm fished in low water really does work like a charm!

Materials

Hook	Low water salmon 'iron' size 6.
Tying thread	Black.
Tag	Oval silver tinsel.
Tail	Golden pheasant topping (crest) feather.
Body	Black floss silk.
Rib	Oval silver tinsel.
Throat hackle	Blue cock.
Wing	Grey squirrel tail.

Tying Details

Take the foundation layer down to the bend of the hook for a high-water version, or just two-thirds of the way to the bend for the low-water fly depicted here. Tie in a length of oval silver tinsel and return the tying thread up the shank to the head position. Tie in a length of black floss, winding it down the shank and back to the head position. Secure the floss and trim off the excess.

Wrap four turns of the silver tinsel around the hook shank to form a silver tag; then rib the body in six equally spaced spiral turns. Secure the tinsel ribbing at the head position and trim off any excess. Now select a bunch

Peter Ross: the finished fly.

Blue Charm: the finished fly.

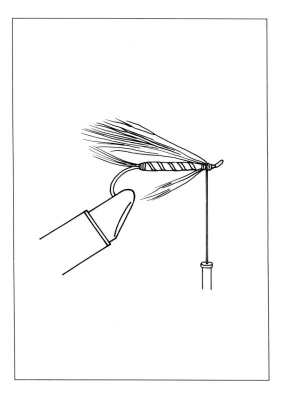

Fig 55   Blue Charm: adding the wing.

of blue cock hackle fibres two-thirds the length of the hook shank and tie them in as a false beard hackle. Complete the fly by tying in the squirrel tail wing using fibres which just reach to the bend of the hook. Add a neat head, whip finish and varnish to complete the Blue Charm.

Tying Tip

For low-water salmon fishing, tie the wing and beard hackle very sparse. Extend the dressing in length and in density of materials if you intend fishing heavier waters.

A TEAL WING FLY – PETER ROSS

Brainchild of a Scottish shopkeeper, for generations the Peter Ross has been popular with both lake and river fishers. We have included it in the wet fly selection because many fly tyers have difficulty with teal wings, whose fibres easily become unmeshed if not handled carefully.

The barred teal feather is an ideal material for fry imitators – flies which are meant to copy small fish, many of which have alternating light and dark vertical bars. Several other famous trout flies make use of barred teal feathers, including the Teal and Red, Teal and Green, and Teal, Blue and Silver, as well as Hugh Falkus' highly successful sea trout fly, Medicine.

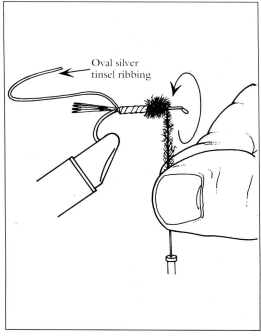

Fig 56   Peter Ross: dubbing the body.

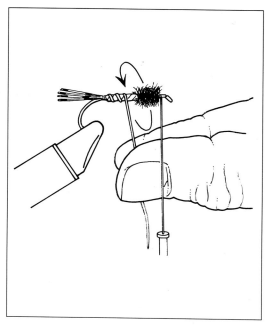

Fig 57 Peter Ross: ribbing the body.

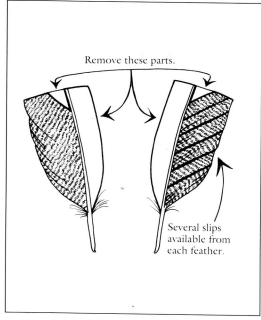

Fig 58 Peter Ross: preparing the wing slips.

Materials

Hook	Down-eye size 10 (6 to 14).
Tying thread	Black.
Tail	Golden pheasant tippets.
Body	Front third of scarlet seal fur or red wool. rear two-thirds of flat silver tinsel.
Rib	Silver oval tinsel.
Hackle	Black cock or hen.
Wing	Barred teal.

Tying Details

Take the foundation layer down to the bend of the hook, and there tie in four well-marked tippet fibres as a tail. Also at the tail position, tie in lengths of body and ribbing tinsel. Take the tying thread two-thirds of the way along the body before winding the flat silver tinsel to the same point. Lock down the flat tinsel and trim off the excess.

The next stage is to dub on the seal fur and wind the front third of the body. Complete the body of the Peter Ross by winding six equally spaced turns of ribbing on top of both sections of the body. Secure the ribbing and trim off the excess.

Wind on just two turns of hackle, angled backwards in the normal wet fly way, and you are ready to fit the teal wing.

The wing slips will, of course, be longer than you need; so tie them in, as a pair, with the butts overlapping the eye of the hook to give the wing length you need. Use the normal pinch-and-loop method to secure the wings, snip off the excess teal feather butts,

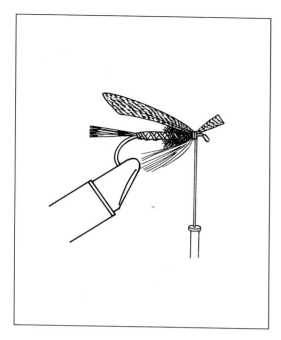

Fig 59 Peter Ross: fitting the barred teal wing.

and add a neat head. Whip finish and varnish to complete the Peter Ross.

Tying Tip

Here is a simple method of handling the teal winging material. Select a matching (left and right) pair of barred teal feathers, and spray them lightly with hair lacquer – this will help keep the fibres married together. Snip off the tips of the feathers to leave a 'V', and then remove all the fibres from the inside of each feather, leaving the longer (outside) fibres attached to the stalk. To make matched wing slips, it is a simply a matter of snipping the required length of stalk from each feather.

MIXING AND MATCHING

The techniques used in tying the flies discussed in this chapetr will allow you to produce numerous other patterns. For example, the pheasant tippet tail and teal wing of the Peter Ross can be combined with the silver body of the Butcher to produce a fly called the Teal Blue and Silver. In fact, there is a family of 'Teal plus something else' flies, including Teal and Red and Teal and Green.

Teal Blue and Silver

This is not only a popular fly for wild trout on lakes and rivers, but one of the most successful sea trout patterns for fishing in fast or slightly coloured water

Materials

Hook	Size 10 (Partridge G3A).
Tying thread	Black.
Tail	Pheasant tippets.
Body	Flat silver tinsel.
Rib	Oval silver tinsel.
Wing	Barred teal flank feathers.

The photographs on the next page show the wing being secured in place and the finished fly.

Tying Tip

For sea trout fishing in low water, shorten the tail to half the length shown in the illustrations on page 82 and reduce the length of the wing so it doesn't extend beyond the hook bend. You will suffer less from 'short takes'.

Teal Blue and Silver: fitting the teal wing.

Teal Blue and Silver: the finished fly.

One way of learning to tie flies is to join a fly-tying class.

8 Dry Flies

For many fly fishers there is a special satisfaction in deceiving a trout with a floating fly. Perhaps this is due, in part, to the anticipation as the fly rests inert upon the surface. In calm clear water, as you see the trout on its way up to inspect your fly, there is also that 'will he; won't he' uncertainty. Whatever the reason, an increasing number of stillwater anglers are following the example of their stream fisher colleagues and switching to the dry fly whenever conditions present an opportunity. For this reason, we have included both river and lake patterns in this selection of dry flies, which make use of a range of traditional and modern materials.

Tying Tip

To lift and spread the tails of a dry fly slightly, do not trim off the spare end of the foundation thread. Instead, once the tail fibres have been secured, pull back on the spare end of thread as you pass the bobbin thread twice beneath the tails but on top of the hook bend. In this way you can keep tension on the tying thread to ensure that the tails remain in place during the spreading process. Finally, trim off the spare end of the foundation thread.

HACKLED DRY FLY – GREY DUSTER

Like the Coch-y-Bonddhu, the Grey Duster is a very old and highly regarded Welsh pattern. It probably ranks second only to the Greenwell's Glory in popularity as a general purpose dry pattern. We use it as an imitation of the egg-laying stoneflies in autumn; but we will admit that most days it is just as readily taken by trout feeding on upwinged duns.

Materials

Hook	Up-eye size 12 (10 to 14).
Tail	Badger cock fibres.
Tying thread	Black.
Body	Grey mole fur.
Hackle	Badger cock hackle.

Tying Tip

Choose a badger cock hackle with nice strong markings, as this will result in a 'bi-visible' fly – when under the shade of trees the light hackle tips will show up clearly, and in bright sunlight the dark centre of the hackle will stand out well against the background of the sparkling water.

Tying Details

Wind the foundation layer and tie in four badger cock hackle fibres as a tail. Dub on the mole fur making a carrot-shaped fly body. Tie in a badger cock hackle and wind on four turns, securing with two pinch-and-loop turns of tying thread. Trim off the excess hackle stalk.

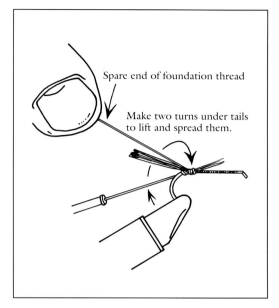

Fig 60 Grey Duster: fitting the (optional) badger cock hackle tail.

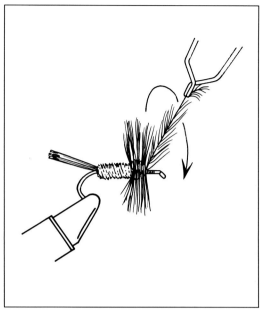

Fig 62 Grey Duster: winding the hackle.

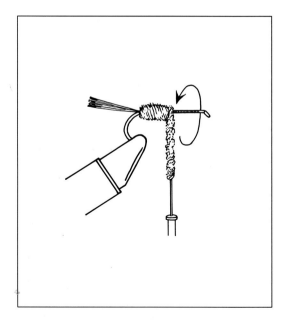

Fig 61 Grey Duster: dubbing the fur body.

Complete the Grey Duster by winding a neat head, whip finishing, and applying two coats of varnish to the head. A simple, but very effective, dry fly.

HACKLED DRY FLY – CUL DE CANARD BLUE DUN

Popular on the Continent for many years, the Cul de Canard patterns make use of the highly buoyant feathers from around the duck's oil gland. This is a relatively expensive material, because one bird provides no more than a couple of dozen feathers. Tied in the method described below, you will find this delicate material becomes surprisingly durable, so your Cul de Canard flies should last well.

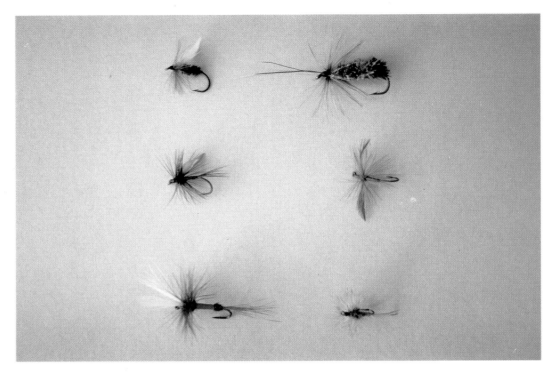

Traditional and modern dry flies. Top row: Coachman, DH Sedge. Middle row: Black Gnat, Sherry Spinner. Bottom Row: Royal Wulff, Grey Duster.

Materials

Hook	Down-eye size 12.
Tying thread	Black.
Tail	Iron-blue dun cock hackle fibres.
Body	Primrose tying thread.
Hackle	Mixed Cul de Canard and iron-blue dun cock.

Tying Details

Wind on a foundation layer of tying thread from head to tail positions. For the tail, tie in six iron-blue dun cock hackle fibres, and then run the tying thread forward in neat touching turns to the head position. The next stage is to tie in the hackle feathers. First tie in the iron-blue dun but do not wind it on. Then tie in the Cul de Canard.

> ### Tying Tip
>
> Instead of tying in the butt of the Cul de Canard feather, which has a rather stiff and unmanageable stalk, tie it in at the tip.

Wind on three turns of Cul de Canard, securing the butt with two pinch-and-loop turns. Trim off the excess stalk. Now wind one turn of the iron-blue behind the Cul de Canard hackle, then bring it through to the front and add a second turn of iron-blue dun hackle. This cock hackle will reinforce the buoyant Cul de Canard, giving you the best

Grey Duster: the finished fly.

of both worlds: excellent buoyancy and good durability.

HACKLE-WINGED DRY FLY – DADDY-LONG-LEGS

August and September are the traditional months for fishing the Daddy-Long-Legs; but, if there is a good breeze and a bit of sunshine, these ungainly fliers (mostly of terrestrial origin) get blown on to the water in large enough numbers to bring trout up throughout the season. With care it is possible to create a very close imitation of this insect, although its struggling antics in the surface film are not so easy to mimic. Nevertheless, twitched in the surface or fished just sub-surface near the margins of lakes, the artificial Daddy-Long-Legs is a most effective fly and we would not be without an imitation.

For stillwater use, a size 10 long-shank hook is fine for autumn fishing; also try smaller versions for fishing in spring when some of the smaller aquatic species of crane flies emerge, or for casting to wild brown trout on upland streams.

Materials

Hook	Down-eye long shank size 10 (10 to 14).
Tying thread	Brown.
Under body	Ethafoam strip.
Over body	Brown raffene varnish.
Rib	Brown tying thread.
Legs	Cock pheasant centre tail fibres.

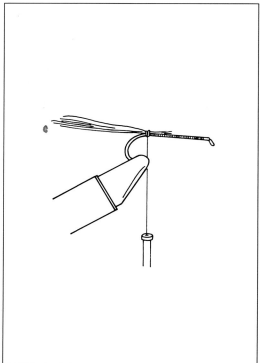

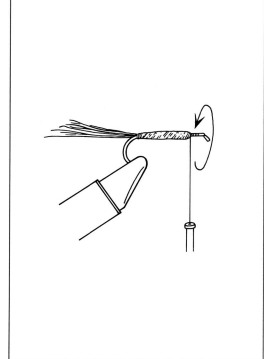

Fig 63   Cul de Canard dun: tying the tail.

Fig 64   Cul de Canard dun: winding the body.

Wings	Grizzle or cree cock hackle tips.
Hackle	Ginger cock hackle.

Tying Details

The first stage is to prepare the legs by tying two knots in each of six pheasant tail fibres.

For the body and ribbing you will need a thin strip of ethafoam about ⅛in. wide and ¹⁄₁₆in. thick, a length of brown raffene (plastic raffia) and a length of brown thread. Tie these three items in all together at the bend of the hook, and then run the tying thread forward to the head position. Wind the ethafoam underbody in touching turns, locking it down

Tying Tip

Tie up enough legs to make a batch of Daddy-Long-Legs. Make a loop in a fibre where you want a leg joint to be, and then use your dubbing needle to ease one end of the fibre through the loop to make an overhand knot. This is much easier than trying to complete the knots with your fingers.

at the head. Now wet the raffene – it is best to use your fingers for this job – and stretch it tightly before winding it along the body on top of the ethafoam. Raffene stretches when

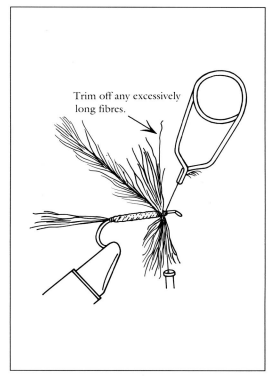

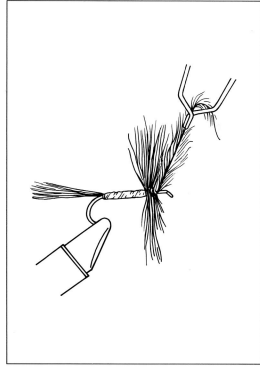

Fig 65 Cul de Canard dun: tying in the CDC hackle.

Fig 66 Cul de Canard dun: winding the blue dun hackle through the CDC hackle.

it is wet, so you will get a tighter, more durable body. Next, you should rib the body by winding the brown thread in the opposite direction to the one used to wind the other body materials, and tie in the legs facing backwards beneath the body.

In order to make the wings, tie in two ginger cock hackle tips, setting them in the spent position by means of figure-of-eight turns of tying thread. Wind on the ginger cock hackle and add a small head to complete the Daddy-Long-Legs. To improve the durability of this fly once it is finished, give both the head and the body a thorough coat of clear varnish.

DEER HAIR DRY FLY – DH SEDGE

Derek Hoskin devised this pattern to copy the many mottled sedges, such as the Grouse Wing. It is an excellent deceiver of lake trout, especially during the evening rise.

On calm water, you only need to fish it stationary or with just an occasional twitch; however on evenings when there is a gentle breeze rippling across the water surface, drag the DH Sedge steadily across the waves and be ready for some truly crashing takes!

It is an action which has resulted in the downfall of countless game fish world-wide.

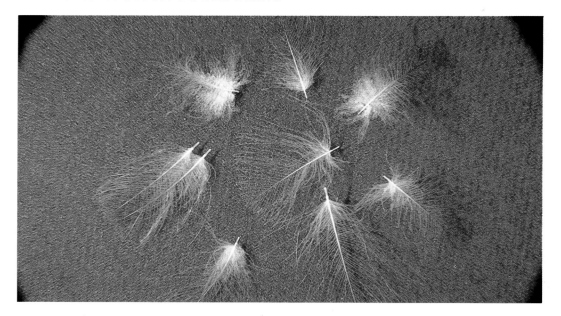

Cul de Canard feathers.

Cul de Canard dun: the finished fly.

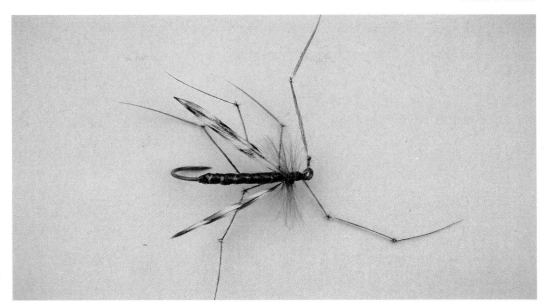

Daddy-long-legs: the finished fly.

DH Sedge: the body ready for trimming.

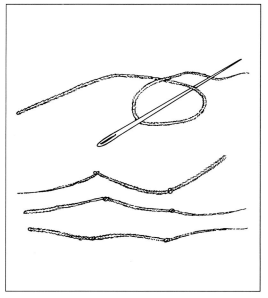

Fig 67 Daddy-long-legs: preparing the legs.

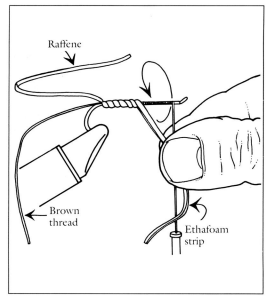

Fig 68 Daddy-long-legs: tying the under-body.

Fig 69 Daddy-long-legs: tying in the legs.

Materials

Hook	Down-eye size 10 (8 to 12).
Tying thread	Black.
Body	Spun deer hair, in dark brown and natural tan.
Wings	Clipped to shape from deer hair.
Hackle	Ginger cock.
Antennae	Badger fibres or stripped cock hackles.

Tying Details

This fly uses the spinning technique to build up the body and wings, which are simply clipped to the familiar shape of a sedge fly at rest.

Begin by winding a foundation layer from the eye to the bend of the hook. Now cut a

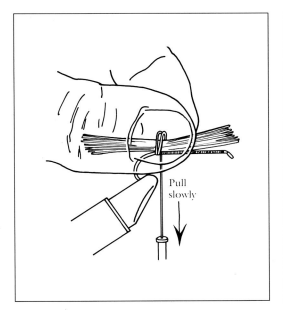

Fig 70 DH Sedge: spinning the deer hair body.

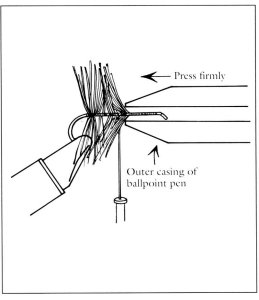

Fig 71 DH Sedge: compacting the spun sections.

bunch of tan deer hair fibres away from the skin, ensure the tips are even, and lay the bunch along the top of the hook shank. Make two loose turns around the shank and over the deer hair at the hook bend. Pull tight slowly, so that the deer hair spins around the shank. Wind the tying thread forward

Tying Tip

The outer plastic tube from a ball-point pen is an ideal tool for pushing back the fibres evenly.

through the fibres and pull the butts of the deer hair back before winding three turns of tying thread around the shank in front of the bunch of flared deer hair.

Now take a bunch of the dark deer hair fibres, hold it over the hook shank, and spin it on in the manner described above. Again bring the tying thread forward and make

Tying Tip
You will probably find it easier to clip the body to shape if you hold the hook in your fingers, gripping the point and the barb. For the final touches, fit the fly back into the vice, where you can rotate it easily to check for symmetry.

three turns in front of the deer hair whilst holding the fibres back. Continue building up sections of light and dark deer hair until you reach a position ⅛in. from the hook eye.

You are now ready to begin clipping the deer hair to shape. Keep the fibres short

DH Sedge: the finished fly.

underneath the hook, so that the gape is not unduly reduced, and taper the underbody down towards the rear. Clip the sides and top of the sedge into a ridge shape, rounding off at the rear to represent the triangular trailing edge of the wings of the natural sedge.

The next step is to tie in the antennae. A pair of badger fibres are ideal but, for those who have not been able to collect this material from roadside casualties, a suitable substitute can be made from cock hackles. Simply strip away the fibres from both sides of a pair of hackles, trimming off the fine tip and tying in at the butts to leave the antennae protruding about 1in beyond the eye of the hook.

To complete the DH Sedge, add two turns of ginger cock hackle, wind a small, neat head and secure the tying with a whip finish. For the finishing touch, apply two coats of varnish to the head.

OTHER OPPORTUNITIES FOR DEER HAIR

Deer hair is such a versatile material, especially for heads and bodies where it can be clipped to shape and, if necessary, bleached and then re-coloured using marker pens.

The Muddlers

Since Don Gapen invented the original Muddler Minnow, fly tyers throughout the world have experimented with other deer hair variants to create realistic imitations of small creatures.

The example on page 95 was tied by Peter Gathercole; it is called the Hen Hackle Muddler. If you want to try a muddler of your own, you must stop the body dressing well short of the eye so there is room to spin on the deer hair.

The Hen Hackle Muddler.

The Deer Hair Perch Fry.

Perch Fly

Also shown above is a perch fry imitation tied with bleached deer hair. With care, you can produce quite a realistic imitation of this little fish. Maybe you could try a grasshopper or a stag beetle in dyed deer hair; remember to use waterproof pens, though!

9 Lures

Small fish, frogs and other swimming creatures may be imitated by a lure. Some successful lure patterns do not copy living creatures at all; they were invented by trial and error, and one can only conclude that they trigger off the predatory instincts in the trout.

Salmon and sea trout flies can also be considered as lures, but in their case they trigger a reaction from fish which rarely feed in fresh water. Protection of personal territory, or even simple curiosity, may be reasons why these migratory fish take our flies; the bright array of colours in so many traditional salmon flies may have evolved because they arouse intense curiosity in the quarry . . . an intriguing thought!

A SEA TROUT LURE – DYFFRYN PEARL

Derek Hoskin developed this night-fishing pattern to reflect the moonlight from the many facets of its mylar wings. It is not only an effective fly for bright nights, but can also be fished with confidence in almost total darkness – somehow the sea trout manage to find it!

Materials

Hook	Double, size 10 (10 to 14).
Butt thread	White.
Head thread	Black.
Tail	Luminous red lureflash.
Body	Fine silver mylar tubing.
Throat hackle	Soft (henny) red hackle.
Underwing	Four strands of pearl mylar, taken from woven tubing.
Overwing	Black squirrel tail.

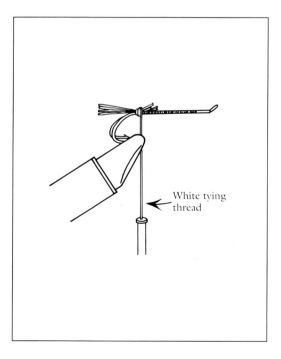

White tying thread

Fig 72 Dyffryn Pearl: fitting a Lureflash tail.

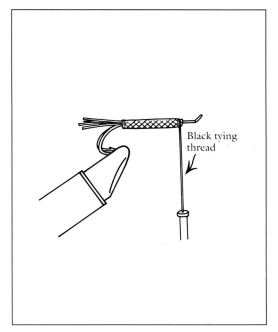

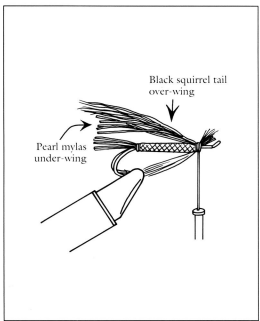

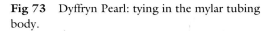

Fig 73 Dyffryn Pearl: tying in the mylar tubing body.

Fig 74 Dyffryn Pearl: tying in the black squirrel over-wing.

Tying details

Cut off the required length of mylar tubing, which will act as the body and remove the inner core. Use the white thread to wind a foundation layer and tie in the lureflash tail. Slide the mylar tubing over the eye of the hook and tie it in at the tail position. Whip finish and apply a coat of clear varnish to the tail thread. Once the varnish has hardened, start again at the head, tying down the mylar tubing and adding a red throat hackle.

Tying Tip

Don't discard the material from the centre of the mylar tubing as it makes excellent dry fly wings e.g. for mayflies in place of the traditional fan wings.

You are now ready to wing your fly. The underwing material is obtained by unravelling a length of the mylar tubing and selecting the pearl strands. Use a pair of 3in lengths tied in at the middle. Fold back the forward facing strands of mylar strip to create a four-strand underwing. Secure with a further three turns of tying thread. On top of the pearl mylar underwing, tie in a sparse overwing of dyed black squirrel tail. A neat head and two coats of varnish complete the fly.

During the summer, when sea trout often take 'short', you should reduce the length of the body of the fly so that it finishes two-thirds of the way along the hook shank instead of at the bend. Ensure that you keep the tail short as well, and you will increase your chances of hooking some of those lazy fish which merely follow and nip at your fly on July nights.

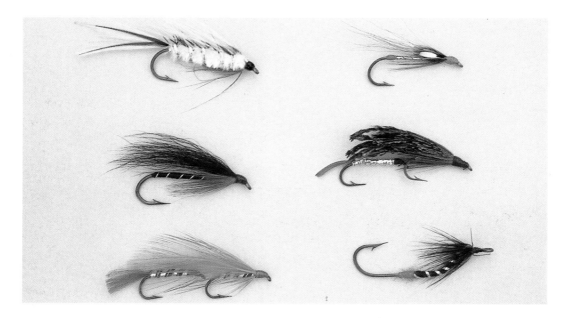

Lures come in all shapes and sizes. Top row: Badger Matuka, Whiskey – Jungle Cock Cheeks. Middle row: Sweeney Todd, Tandem Alexandra. Bottom row: Tandem Whiskey, Dyffryn Demon.

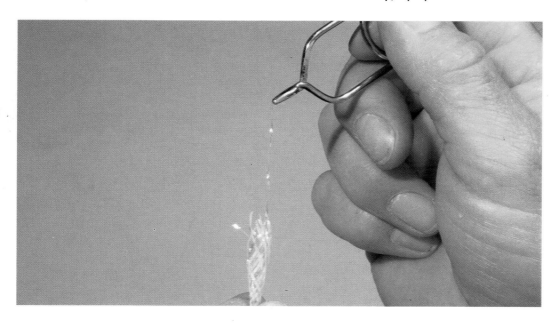

Dyffryn Pearl: preparing the mylar.

Dyffryn Pearl: the finished fly.

Garry: the finished tube fly.

A TUBE FLY – GARRY (YELLOW DOG)

A popular salmon fly for many decades, the original contained hair taken from a golden retriever. This tube version will take both salmon and sea trout, and it is particularly effective when the water is slightly stained with peat.

Materials

Hook	Size 10 (8 to 14) treble.
Tying thread	Black.
Body tube	11/2in polythene, aluminium or brass tube.
Tag	Oval tinsel.
Butt	Yellow silk floss.
Body	Black silk floss.
Rib	Oval silver tinsel.
Underwing	A few fibres of red bucktail.
Overwing	Yellow bucktail.
Head hackle	Dyed blue guinea-fowl.

Tying Details

Plastic tubes can be bought, or can be made from spent ball-point pen inners. Ready-made metal tubes with belled ends and plastic inserts are also obtainable at reasonable prices, and they are very easy to handle. However, if you do decide to make your own metal tubes, use the point of a drill bit to remove any burrs. This is essential to avoid chafing the nylon which passes through the middle of the tube.

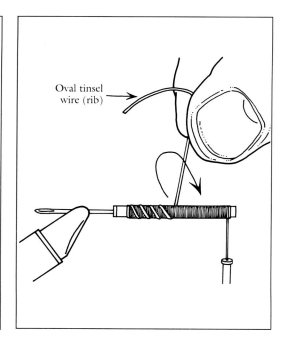

Fig 75   Garry: tying in the body and rib materials.

Fig 76   Garry: ribbing the body.

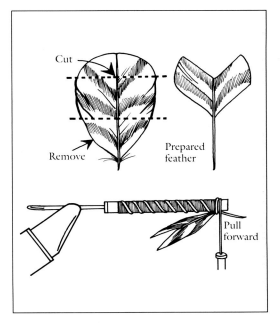

Fig 77   Garry: tying in the throat hackle.

Tying Tip

Tools which are simple but very effective are available for securing tubes to the tying vice. These are inexpensive and worth getting if you intend tying a lot of tube flies.

Jam the tube on to a needle of suitable diameter, and fix the needle securely in the tying vice.

Wind on a foundation layer. Now tie in the tag, using four turns of the oval silver tinsel, followed by a butt consisting of three turns of yellow floss silk. Add in the body floss and ribbing materials before running the thread back to the head end. Wind a slim body with touching turns of floss, lock down the floss at the head and trim off any excess. Rib the body

Tying Tip

On larger tubes it is neater and easier, having removed the flue from the base of the guinea-fowl feather, to cut and discard the tip, and tie in the feather at the throat position using three turns of thread. Now pull the feather stalk forward gently until you obtain the desired length of fibres. Add two more turns of thread to secure and trim off the loose ends.

with well-spaced turns, and secure the ribbing at the head. Next add a throat hackle using a generous bunch of blue guinea fowl fibres.

Now for the wing. Select a sparse bunch of red bucktail and spread the fibres around the head of the tube. Secure the underwing with three turns of tying thread. Repeat the process with a more generous bunch of yellow bucktail for the overwing.

Finally, make a secure whip finish. Apply two coats of varnish and allow to dry. Remove the needle and the Garry is ready to accept its treble hook.

Tying Tip

As additional camouflage for the hook, two turns of short black hackle can be wound on to the shank of the treble hook. Take care when you are whip finishing this tying that you keep your fingers clear of the hook points.

MARABOU LURE – VIVA

This is a variation on the original Viva, invented by Victor Furse. We have dispensed with the mixed wing of marabou and squirrel

Viva: tying in the marabou plume.

Viva: the finished fly.

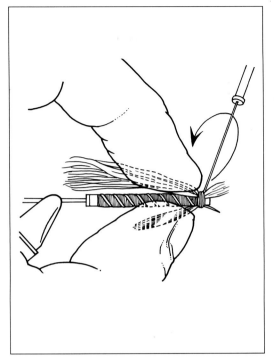

Fig 78 Garry: adding the hair wing.

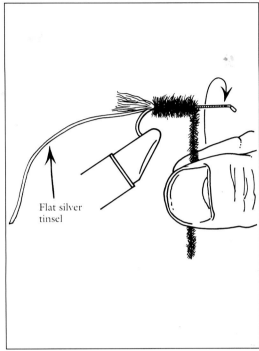

Flat silver tinsel

Fig 79 Viva: winding the chenille body.

tail, using marabou alone for the wing material. The green tail, sometimes tied as a short tag, seems to be the thing that initially attracts the attention of the trout; so, if the water is none too clear, fit a sizeable tail of green fluorescent wool.

Materials

Hook	Down-eye long shank 10 (8 to 12).
Tying thread	Black.
Tag	Green fluorescent wool No. 12.
Body	Black chenille.
Rib	Flat silver tinsel.
Wing	Black marabou plume.

Tying Details

Once you have wound the foundation thread down to the hook bend, tie in a bunch of fluorescent green wool to act as a tail. Next tie in the flat silver tinsel and, having removed the flue from the last ⅛in, add in the black chenille. Take the tying thread back to the head position.

Now wind the chenille tightly along the hook shank to create the body of the fly, and rib it in well-spaced turns, winding the flat silver tinsel in the opposite direction to the one used for the chenille. Carefully secure and trim off any waste body and ribbing materials. The fly is now ready to have its marabou wings fitted.

103

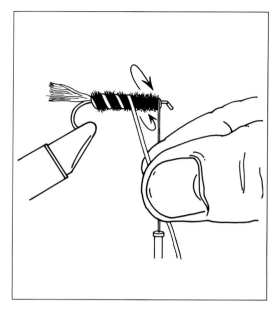

Fig 80   Viva: ribbing the body.

Tying Tip

Marabou can be difficult to handle, but here is an idea which will make it more manageable. Pull the marabou herls at right angles to the feather stalk, peel them away from the stalk and wet the fingers of your free hand. With your wet fingers, grip the butts of the marabou herls and twist them together in a bunch. It will be much easier to tie the wet butts down if you handle them in this way.

Use three pinch-and-loop turns to secure the marabou wing in place. Trim off the spare butt material before finishing with a neat head. Whip finish and varnish the head of the Viva to complete it.

Glossary

Abdomen The segmented rear section of an insect's body.

Badger hackle A hackle having a black centre and white outer fibres, sometimes tipped with black.

Barb The backward-facing projection cut into a hook near the point to reduce the chances of a hooked fish escaping. Barbless hooks have been shown to achieve similar results.

Bi-visible A fly with both light and dark coloured hackles to give good visibility in both light and shaded water.

Blue dun hackle A slate-blue or grey hackle.

Bucktail Deer tail. Also fry-imitating lures tied with deer hair wings.

Cape The neck of poultry or game birds, from whence hackle feathers are obtained.

Chenille A furry, rope-like material used for lure bodies.

Coch-y-bonddhu hackle A hackle with black centre and red edges tipped with black.

Cock hackles The neck feathers of a cockerel.

Cree hackle A barred black, red and ginger hackle, sometimes with cream or white flecks.

Cul de Canard An extremely buoyant feather from around the oil gland near the base of a duck's tail.

Detached body Fly bodies tied not around the shank of the hook but attached only at the head of the fly.

Diptera Two-winged, or 'true', flies, including the daddy-long-legs and midges.

Dry fly A fly designed to float on the surface of the water.

Dubbing The technique of spinning fur on to waxed thread and winding it around a hook shank to make a fly body.

Dun The first winged stage of an upwinged insect.

Dun hackle A greyish brown hackle.

Ephemeroptera Upwinged flies and their nymphs.

Ethafoam A synthetic material useful for making floating flies.

Floss Multi-strand silk or synthetic substitute used in making fly bodies.

Fluorescent Material which emits light of a visible colour when ultra-violet light falls upon it.

Furnace hackle A hackle with a black centre and red edges.

Golden Pheasant Gamebird whose crest, neck and wing feathers are used extensively in fly patterns.

Greenwell hackle A hackle with a red centre and ginger edges.

Grizzle hackle A hackle with black and white bars (as Plymouth Rock).

Hackle A neck feather tied to represent the legs of an insect.

Herl The individual fibres of a feather (especially ostrich and peacock) used as tail and body materials.

Honey dun hackle A brown hackle with light ginger edges.

Ibis Red feathers used as tails of flies. Substitutes include dyed swan and goose wing feathers.

Jungle cock An Indian game bird whose hackles have distinctive cream 'eye' markings.

Lurex A plastic material available in many colours including gold and silver, used as a substitute for tinsel.

Marabou Turkey feather fibres used extensively as wings and tails of lures.

Mylar Metallic plastic available in sheet or plaited tube form. The tubing can be used to simulate scales on the flanks of fry-imitating lures.

Order A sub-division of the class of insects. Most of the flies of interest to anglers and fly tyers fall within the orders Ephemeroptera, Tricoptera, Diptera and Plecoptera.

Palmer A hackle wound spirally along the body of a fly.

Parachute fly A fly with its hackle wound in the horizontal plane.

Plastazote Buoyant plastic material similar to ethafoam.

Plymouth Rock hackle A hackle with grey centre and bands of black and white.

Polypropylene Synthetic material available in very fine fibres suitable for dubbing, or in coarser strands which can serve as wing or tail materials.

Polyvinyl chloride (PVC) An almost clear, Soft plastic used to create translucent bodies.

Plecoptera Stoneflies and their nymphs.

Spinner The final adult stage of an upwinged insect.

Spent gnat A fly which has laid her eggs and is dead or dying on the surface of the water.

Tandem lure A lure consisting of two or more in-line hooks connected by short lengths of strong nylon.

Thorax   The front portion of the body of an insect to which the wings and legs are attached.

Tippet   A small orange-and-black barred feather from the golden pheasant.

Topping   A curved narrow gold feather from the crest of a golden pheasant.

Tricoptera   Sedge or caddis flies, their nymphs and pupae.

Tube fly   A lure tied on a plastic or metal tube, used in salmon and sea trout fishing.

Wet fly   An artificial fly designed to swim beneath the water surface.

Whip finish   A knot which is used to secure the tying thread upon completion of the head of a fly.

Whisks   The individual filaments tied to represent the tails or setae of an insect.

Wing case   The hump containing the developing wings on the back of a nymph nearing maturity.

Useful Addresses

The Fly Dressers' Guild
Errol A. Walling (Membership Secretary),
29 Windmill Hill, Ruislip,
Middlesex HA4 8PY, UK.

Salmon and Trout Association
Fishmongers' Hall, London Bridge, London
EC4R 9EL, UK. Tel: 071 283 5838.

Scottish Anglers' National Assembly
Mr Mike Shanks (Honorary Secretary),
Craiganrioch, Kilkerran Road,
Campbelltown, Argyl, UK. Tel: 0586
54243.

Welsh Salmon & Trout Angling Association
Mr Moc Morgan (Honorary Secretary),
Swyn Teifi, Pontrhydfendigaid, Ystrad
Meurin, Dyfed SY25 6BB, UK. Tel: 09745
316.

The Anglers' Co-operative Association
23 Castlegate, Grantham, Lincolnshire
NG31 6SW, UK. Tel: 0746 61008.

CENTRES FOR FLY TYING TUITION

Many local education authorities provide
evening classes, usually starting in September.
Some fly fishing schools also offer tuition:

West Wales School Of Flyfishing
Ffoshelyg, Lancych, Boncath, Dyfed SA37
0LJ, UK. Tel: 023977 678.

SUPPLIERS OF HOOKS, TOOLS AND MATERIALS

Partridge of Redditch (Hook makers)
Mount Pleasant, Redditch, West Midlands
B97 4JE, UK. Tel: 0527 43555.

Mustad (Hook makers)
2 Brindley Road, Peterlee, Co. Durham SR8
2LT, UK. Tel: 091 5869533.

Piscatoria (Fly tying tools)
3A Hebden Court, Bakewell, Derbyshire,
UK. Tel: 062981 4770.

Fishermen's Feathers
Hillend Farm, Station Road, Bransford,
Worcestershire WR6 5JU, UK. Tel: 0905
830548.

Lureflash Products (Tools, hooks and
materials)
10 Adwick Road, Mexborough, South
Yorkshire, S64 0AW, UK. Tel: 0709
580238.

Campbell Black & Co (Tools, hooks and
materials)
Rood End House, 6 Stortford Road, Great
Dunmow, Essex CM6 1DA, UK. Tel: 0371
873595.

Further Reading

FLY TYING

Dawes, M.,	*The Fly Tyer's Manual* (Collins, 1985).
Gathercole, P.,	*The Handbook of Fly Tying* (The Crowood Press, 1989).
O'Reilly, P.,	*Fishing Facts – Fly Tying* (The Crowood Press, 1991).
Wakeford, J.,	*Flytying Techniques* (A & C Black, 1980).

FLY PATTERNS

Church, R.,	*Guide to Trout Flies* (The Crowood Press, 1987).
Price, T.,	*Fly Patterns – An International Guide* (Ward Lock, 1986).
Roberts, J.,	*The New Illustrated Dictionary of Trout Flies* (Allen and Unwin, 1986).
Roberts, J.,	*A Guide to River Trout Flies* (The Crowood Press, 1989).
Stewart, T.,	*Two Hundred Popular Flies And How To Tie Them* (Benn, 1979).
Williams, A.C.,	*A Dictionary of Trout Flies* (A & C Black, 1949).

TROUT FLY IDENTIFICATION

Goddard, J.,	*Trout Fly Recognition* (A & C Black, 1966).
Goddard, J.,	*Trout Flies of Stillwater* (A & C Black, 1975).
Harris, J. R.,	*An Angler's Entomology* (Collins, 1952).

FLY SELECTION AND FISHING TACTICS

Church, B. and Gathercole, P.,	*Imitations of the Trout's World* (The Crowood Press, 1985).
Clarke, B. and Goddard, J.,	*The Trout and the Fly* (Benn, 1980).
O'Reilly, P.,	*Tactical Fly Fishing* (The Crowood Press, 1990).
Roberts, J.,	*To Rise a Trout* (The Crowood Press, 1988).
Sawyer, F.,	*Nymphs and the Trout* (A & C Black, 1974).

Index

Alexandra 98

Badger Matuka 98
Barb faults 17
Beard hackle 48
Beetles 57
Bench 12
Bi-visible fly 84
Black And Peacock Spider 36
Black Gnat 15, 86
Blending furs 61
Blue Charm 76
Blue Winged Olive 54
Bobbin holder 13
Bodies
  chenille 36
  deer hair 37
  feather fibre 32
  fur 35, 37
  mylar 35, 37
  peacock herl 36
  ribbing 32, 34
  silk floss 31
  thread 30
Butcher 73
Buzzer 65, 68

Caddis 59
Capes 22, 47
Carnill, R 69
Chenille 22, 63
Chironomids 56, 68
Coachman 86
Coch-y-bonddhu 22, 84
Colour matching 57

Connemara Black 74
Craft knife 14, 36
Cul de Canard 85, 90

Daddy-Long-Legs 87
Damsel nymph 59
Deer hair bodies 37
DH Sedge 89
Double hooks 21
Dry flies 84
Dubbing
  bodies 37
  loop 36
  needle 14
  tool 36
Dyffryn Demon 98
Dyffryn Pearl 97

Ephemeroptera 56
Ethafoam 65, 87

Falkus, H 79
Feathers
  fibres 32
  storage 21
  types 22
Flies, natural
  classification 52
  midge 56
  sedge 55
  stonefly 56
  upwinged 54
Foundation layer 26
Furs 22
Furze, V 101

G & H Sedge 38
Gallena 73
Gapen, D 94
Garry 100
Gathercole, P 94
Grannom 71
Greenwell's Glory 7, 84
Grey Duster 84

Hackle pliers 13
Hackles
  cockerel 22
  collar 48
  hen 22
  palmering 48, 71
  storage 21
  throat 45, 48
Hair
  bodies 37
  tails 28
Heads 29
Hooks
  barbless 24
  dimensions 25
  faults 17
  profiles 20
  quality 16
  storage 19
  testing 16
  treble 100

Insects 55
Invicta 71

Jungle Cock 41, 98

Kite's Imperial 7, 54

Lighting 12
Linsell, K 57
Lures 96

Magnifiers 9, 12
Mallard And Claret 71

Marabou 28, 101, 104
Materials 15
Matuka 41
Mayfly 58
Medicine 79
Midge 56
Montana nymph 63
Muddlers 38, 94
Mylar 35

Nymphs and pupae 59

Ogden, J 71

Paint 19
Palmering 46, 49, 71
Partridge of Redditch 20
Pens—permanent colouring 19
Peter Ross 7, 79
Pheasant Tail nymph 34
Pinch and loop technique 27
Plastic materials 22
Plecoptera 56
Polythene shrimp shell 61

Red Tag 74
Ribbing 21, 34

Salmon flies 51, 76, 96
Scalpel 14
Scissors 13
Sea trout flies 96
Sedge flies 55
Sedge pupa 64
Sherry Spinner 54
Shrimp 60
Silk floss 22, 31
Spider 57
Spinner 58
  B-w olive 54
  mayfly 58
  sherry 54
Spring, material 13
Stoneflies 44, 56, 84

INDEX

Storage of materials 11, 15
Storage of tools 14
Sweeney Todd 53
Synthetic materials 18, 22

Tails
    hair 28
    feather 26
    marabou 28
Tandem lures 98
Teal, Blue And Silver 71, 81
Teal fly series 79
Terrestrials 56
Thread 18, 30
Tinsels 18, 21
Tools 9, 12
Treble hooks 21, 100
Tricoptera 56
Trigger points 24, 55
Tube flies 100

Upwinged flies 53

Varnishes 19, 22
Vice 13
Viva 53, 101

Water boatman 57
Wax 24
Weighting techniques 60
Wet flies 71
Whip finish 29
Whip finish tool 14, 31
Whiskey 43
Wickham's Fancy 46
Wings
    dry fly 40
    feather slip 40
    hair 42
    hackle point 40
    marabou 103
    matuka 41
    streamer 41
Wing case 33
Wet flies 71
Wool 22
Work area 11
Wulff flies 44, 46
Wulff, L 42

Yellow Dog 100